新理念 雅思口语教程

西安交通大学『十四五』规划教材

主编 编者

钱希 何惠勤 刘帅
杨扬 甄瑞杰
胡洁 彭荣
龚颖

A TRANSFORMATIVE COURSE BOOK:

IELTS SPEAKING

西安交通大学出版社
XI'AN JIAOTONG UNIVERSITY PRESS
国 家 一 级 出 版 社
全国百佳图书出版单位

图书在版编目（CIP）数据

新理念雅思口语教程 / 钱希主编. — 西安：西安交通大
学出版社，2022.2
ISBN 978-7-5693-2344-3

Ⅰ. ①新… Ⅱ. ①钱… Ⅲ. ①IELTS – 口语 – 高等学
校 – 教材 Ⅳ. ①H319.9

中国版本图书馆CIP数据核字(2021)第223141号

XINLINIAN YASI KOUYU JIAOCHENG
新理念雅思口语教程

主　　编	钱　希	
责任编辑	李　蕊	
责任校对	庞钧颖	

出版发行　西安交通大学出版社
　　　　　（西安市兴庆南路1号　邮政编码710048）
网　　址　http://www.xjtupress.com
电　　话　（029）82668357 82667874（市场营销中心）
　　　　　（029）82668315（总编办）
传　　真　（029）82668280
印　　刷　陕西龙山海天艺术印务有限公司

开　　本　850mm×1168mm　1/16　印张　14.5　字数　490千字
版次印次　2022年2月第1版　2022年2月第1次印刷
书　　号　ISBN 978-7-5693-2344-3
定　　价　58.00元

如发现印装质量问题，请与本社市场营销中心联系。
订购热线：（029）82665248　（029）82665249
投稿热线：（029）82668531　（029）82665371

前 言

Preface

　　《国家中长期教育改革和发展规划纲要(2010 — 2020 年)》提出，要"培养大批具有国际视野、通晓国际规则、能够参与国际事务和国际竞争的国际化人才。"英语作为国际化人才的通用语言与交流工具，有助于学生树立世界眼光，培养国际意识，提高人文素养。《新理念雅思口语教程》以主题内容为依托，以口语技能为主线，秉持"以听促说、以读促说、以思促说、以评促说"的原则，将口语作为主要突破口用以提升学生的英语综合能力、思辨能力及用英语讲述中国故事的能力，为其今后的专业深造、职业发展及国际交流提供有效支撑。

　　《新理念雅思口语教程》适合备考雅思的各类考生，也适合希望提升英语口语综合表达能力和思辨能力的高中生、本科生及英语口语基础薄弱的研究生。

本书的编写理念

1. 强调"有效输入促进有效输出"的设计理念

　　本书基于语言输入假说和动态评估理论，注重对口语输出任务的支架搭建，包括有一定挑战度的听力输入和阅读输入等。书中系列任务的设计符合学生认知规律，通过提供渐进干预和指导，引导学生由简到繁、由易到难逐步完成口语产出任务，帮助他们实现从"工具调节"到"他人调节"，再到"自我调节"的飞跃。

2. 注重"自下而上"和"自上而下"的口语训练模式

　　根据认知负荷理论，本书不仅重视"自下而上"词句层面促进口语产出的内容编写，还重视"自上而下"篇章层面和逻辑思维的技能融入与策略训练，目的是帮助学生减轻口语表达中的内在、外在及其相关认知负荷，提升学生口语表达的流利度、连贯性和思想性，从而在雅思口语等考试中做到自如、自信，有内容、有逻辑、有深度地表达。

3. 聚焦雅思口语核心技能与主题，模拟真题开展训练

本书涵盖了雅思等口语考试的核心技能与陈述（交流）主题，对每个单元的各项技能进行了系统性、整体性、科学性的设计与编排，尽量做到单项技能的循序渐进并兼顾多项技能之间的协同发展。模拟真题的训练结合章节主题和核心技能，力图做到"练习代表性强、举例示范度高、讲解针对性强、评价反馈有效"。

4. 全面融入思政元素，培养具有社会主义核心价值观的国际化人才

本书在教材内容选取方面，充分考虑到了"工具性""人文性""国际性"相结合的原则，各章节主题既契合雅思口语考试的高频考点，又充分体现课程的价值导向；在任务设计方面，引导学生开展基于跨文化的、思辨的探讨与实践，在提升学生学术英语口语表达能力的过程中，帮助他们形成科学的思维观、国际化的视野，提升正确的价值判断和选择能力，从而涵养他们兼容并蓄的胸怀与家国情怀。

本书特点

1. 采用"概念教学法"，帮助学生高效掌握相关口语技能

本书基于社会文化理论（Sociocultural Theory）中的概念教学法 (Concept-based Instruction) 进行编写，从学生认知特点和实际需求出发，把抽象的口语技能和思辨技巧等巧妙地转换成生动形象的图式（Schema of Orientation Basic Action，简称 SCOBA），从而有效降低了学生在口语表达过程中的认知负荷，辅助学生实现相关口语知识与技能的内化。

2. 形成性评价设计贯穿始终，注重"以评为学、以评促学、以评促教"理念的系统性实践

本书在每一章节的口语产出部分都设计了学生互评或自评表，鼓励学生在教师引导下开展合作评价与反馈；在任务设计中，采用了选择性答案评价 (selected-response assessment)、结构性答案评价 (constructed-response assessment)、个性化答案评价 (personal-response assessment) 等多种形成性评价方式；每一章节最后都设计了

学生整体性自评与反思表格，强调培养学生的元认知能力。

3. 以国家人才培养需求为导向，强调语言、技能、价值并重

每一章节的单元主题既考虑到了雅思口语考试题目的特点，又巧妙地融入了思政内容。在任务设计中，本书注重引导学生开展研讨式、案例式、辩论式的活动，并且以间接、内隐、柔性的方式融入思政元素，从而完成课程的知识目标、技能目标和价值目标，使三大目标有机融合，形成协同效应。

本书可作为必修课或选修课教材，需要48课内学时。教师在使用过程中，可根据学生或本校实际情况进行筛选或补充。本书的编者们来自西安交通大学外国语学院大学英语教学中心以及新东方教育科技集团国际教育培训事业部，在编写过程中，他们充分利用了扎实的外语教学理论知识和丰富的雅思口语教学经验，使本书兼具学术性和实用性。本书在编写过程中，得到了编者家人、朋友及出版社的大力支持与鼓励，尤其是出版前突遇西安新冠肺炎疫情，雅思口语课程组外教 Brendan 在家隔离期间克服困难录制了本书的部分音频，在此一并表示诚挚的谢意。

Dawn is breaking and we are seeing light coming through.

钱　希

2022 年 1 月于西安

目 录

Contents

CHAPTER 1

Education

LEARNING OBJECTIVES

In this chapter you will learn

- what IELTS Speaking Test is
- how to use signpost language in speaking
- how to express your own opinion
- how to use PPF strategy in IELTS Speaking Test
- the value of educational theories from Confucius and John Dewey

Part One   Warming-up

Task 1   *Please list the concerns if you plan to study abroad. Share ideas with your partners. You may jot down the key words in the following box while preparing for your description.*

```
1.



2.



3.


```

Task 2   *Please list the differences and similarities between Eastern education and Western education in terms of your prior knowledge. You may discuss with your partners and compare your discussion results with other groups.*

NO.	Similarities	Differences
1		
2		
3		
4		

Task 3   *Listen to a short presentation about "the root of learning". Then fill the blanks in the following sentences.*

1. The Chinese characters for learning contain _____. The first character means "_____", and the second character means "_____".

2. As widely known, Chinese characters have been developed from _____.

3. For instance, the first character of "to study" is composed of two parts. ... , and the other part symbolizes "_____".

4. The second character of "to practice repeatedly" is also composed of two parts. ... , and the other part symbolizes "_____", so that it can leave the nest.

5. To summarize, according to ancient Chinese thinking, learning contains the following two elements: (1) to study, i.e. _____ of knowledge; and (2) to practice repeatedly, i.e. _____.

Part Two   IELTS Speaking Test

General Introduction to IELTS Speaking Test

IELTS Speaking Test is a shared module for both Academic and General Versions. The Speaking Module is the final part of the IELTS exam, which is a one-to-one interaction between the candidate and an examiner. It does not need to be taken on the same day as the other Modules. It takes the form of three-part oral interview, which takes between 11 and 14 minutes. The three parts give the candidate the opportunity to use a range of different speaking skills. IELTS Speaking is recorded. Candidates are assessed on their performance throughout the test. The details are shown in Table 1−1.

Table 1−1   General Structure and Content of IELTS Speaking Test

	Time	Content	Ability Tested
Part 1	4–5 minutes	**Introduction and Interview** In the first part, the examiner will ask you a number of general questions. Be prepared to introduce yourself and talk about things which are personal to you, for example, your country and home town, your family, your studies or work, what you like doing in your free time and what you might do in the future.	The ability of daily communication with common topics.
Part 2	3–4 minutes	**Individual Long Turn** In this part, the examiner will give you a card that asks you to talk about a person, place, event or object. You will have 1 minute to prepare to speak, and then you will talk for 1-2 minutes, during which the examiner will not speak. The examiner will then ask one or two rounding-off questions.	The ability of presenting a specific topic in a long run. The ability of using language appropriately and organizing ideas logically and coherently.
Part 3	4–5 minutes	**Two-Way Discussion** In the last part, you will talk with the examiner about issues related to the topic on the card. However, the discussion will be on less personal topics. For example, in Part 2 you may talk about a teacher you had at school, but in Part 3 you might talk about education in your country.	The ability of expressing, analyzing, discussing a topic. The ability of probing into a problem.

Criteria for IELTS Speaking Test

Performance is assessed on the following criteria.

	Detailed Explanation	Ask Yourself
Fluency and Coherence	It refers to the ability to talk with normal levels of communication, rate and effort and to connect ideas and language together to establish a coherent, systematic speech.	Do I express ideas and opinions clearly and coherently, without long hesitations?
Lexical Resource	It refers to the range of vocabulary the interviewees can use and the accuracy with ideas and meanings could be conveyed.	Do I use a wide range of vocabulary?
Grammatical Range and Accuracy	It refers to the range and the accuracy of grammar which interviewees have owned. Words, phrases and sentences would be the key indicators.	Do I use a wide range of structures and make only a few minor mistakes?
Pronunciation	It refers to the clear pronunciation in the whole speaking test. The amount of strain caused to the listener. The tone and intonation will also be the key indicators.	Am I easy to be understood? Do I use English pronunciation features naturally?

IELTS Speaking Skill

Signposts are words, phrases and sentences that let the audience know where the speaker is and what he is going to do. They are used to make a presentation effective, interesting and easy to follow. So it is a good idea to learn a few of the common phrases, which can help your speaking more logic and easy for listeners to follow. The Task 1 includes some signpost language.

Task 1 *Please read the following words and phrases, tell the function of each type of signpost language, and write down in the right column.*

Signpost Language	Function
The subject/topic of my talk is ... My topic today is ... My talk is concerned with ... Let's begin/start by ...	
For example, ... A good example of this is ... To illustrate this point ... ... is a case in point.	
Moving on now to ... Let's turn now to ... The next issue/topic I'd like to focus on ... I'd like to expand/elaborate on ...	
I'm happy to answer any questions. Please feel free to ask questions. Any questions?	
To sum up ... To summarize ... Let's summarize briefly what ... Finally, let me remind you of ... We've covered ... To conclude ... In short ... That's all I have to say about ... So much for ...	
In comparison, ... In contrast, ... Unlike the previous..., ...	
First of all, I'll ... ... and then I'll go on to ... Then/ Next ... Finally/ Lastly ...	
Simply put ... In other words ... To put it another way ...	
Where does that lead us? Let's consider this in more detail ... Translated into real terms ... The significance of this is ...	

Please share your idea with your partners about the following questions. Use proper signposts in your speaking.

1. Should teachers be funny when they teach?
2. What qualities should teachers have?

Part Three　Speaking after Reading

Studying Abroad

Increasing higher education populations have placed enormous pressure on higher education systems of many developing countries. Specifically, the rising number of mobile students is possibly a partial outcome of the worldwide growth of higher education. As Bhandari and Blumenthal claimed, global **student mobility** is a burgeoning phenomenon that affects countries and their academic systems. Most countries currently view international academic mobility and educational exchange as critical components for sharing knowledge, building intellectual capital, and remaining competitive in a globalizing world.

An increasing numbers of students have realized that studying abroad will enhance their career options, when they enter a marketplace that requires knowledge and skills beyond those taught at home. European exchange programs such as the Erasmus Mundus, the U.S. Council on International Educational Student Exchange, and the Euro-American "Atlantis" program all envisage an urgent agenda on how to balance local with more global criteria in higher education. For instance, Erasmus was a trigger for a qualitative leap of internationalization strategies and policies since the 1990s toward cooperation and mobility on equal terms and toward systematic and strategic internationalization.

Global trend

Contemporary higher education has been influenced by two mega-trends—massification and globalization. In the twenty-first century, globalization has had a substantial impact on all of higher education, and simultaneously, massification has influenced the globalized academic environment. The dramatic increase in the number of students studying outside the borders of their home countries is one manifestation of this impact. Globally, the increase in the number of foreign students can be contrasted to the rise in tertiary enrollment. According to UNESCO data, 165 million students participated in formal tertiary education worldwide in 2009; this is an increase of 65 million students since 2000 and a growth of 65 %. The number of foreign students increased during the same period, from 2.1 to 3.7 million students, which is a growth of 77 %. Consequently, the proportion of foreign students among all tertiary students grew by 7 % from 2000 to 2009. Increased international study has numerous causes, one of which is a lack of capacity in home countries, which is an effect of massification. Other international initiatives include the rapid growth of branch campuses, twinning programs, joint degree arrangements, and the franchising of academic programs.

Factors affecting international study

As the Gonzalez shows, they used the determinants of Erasmus student mobility to establish relevant hypotheses. A panel data set of bilateral flows for all participating countries has been used to test the factors influencing student flows. Country size, cost of living, distance, educational background, university quality, host country language, and climate are all found to be significant determinants. Various new institutions and alternative approaches to international study have emerged to meet the growing need for cost-effective education, and consequently, many students are choosing to stay home while also acquiring an international education. These new models of education include distance learning, joint and dual degrees, branch campuses, and sandwich programs involving short-term study abroad. Gray termed these programs ''non-traditional academic arrangements.'' Technology, communication, access to travel, and most importantly the globalized economy have altered how students and educators perceive international study. The information revolution, the global economy and capital market, environmental concerns, and global health and safety have dramatically increased student needs for direct experience abroad.

The effect of economic recession

The global financial recession affected growth in selected sectors, and higher education could still become a potential casualty. Economic globalization has transformed the role of colleges and universities in the Asian region. Rapid expansion has been fueled by an increased demand for higher education that has been fostered by the successful popularization of basic education, rising household expectations, government subscription to the discourse of knowledge economics, human resource needs, and increased availability of distance programs, and private for-profit programs. How this could affect international student mobility? Despite the general trend that student mobility flows from economically less developed toward economically developed countries, the Kondakci study suggests that, in the periphery, regional hubs are attracting students originating largely from other countries within the periphery. The global economic crisis especially the crisis under the impact of COVID-19 has accelerated the need for Asian universities to engage internationally, and to create regional mechanisms through which students and faculty members can move more easily from one country to another.

Adapted from the article written by Dian-Fu Chang published in *Asia Pacific Educ. Rev.*

Word Bank

partial	*adj.* being or affecting only a part; not total 局部的
burgeon	*v.* grow and flourish 迅速增长
trigger	*v.* put in motion or move to act 触发，引起；开动
qualitative	*adj.* involving distinctions based on qualities 质的；定性的
massification	*n.* being popular among the public 大众化
manifestation	*n.* a clear appearance 表现；显示
tertiary	*adj.* at the university or college level 大学的
franchise	*v.* grant a franchise to 给……以特许；授权
hypothesis	*n.* a proposal intended to explain certain facts or observations 假设
emerge	*v.* come out into view, as from concealment 浮现
cost-effective	*adj.* productive relative to the cost 划算的
alter	*v.* cause to change; make different; cause a transformation 改变，更改
perceive	*v.* to become aware of through the senses 感觉；感知；理解
casualty	*n.* someone injured or killed in an accident 意外事故
fuel	*v.* stimulate 推动
subscription	*n.* a payment for consecutive issues of a newspaper or magazine for a given period of time 订阅
periphery	*n.* the outside boundary or surface of something 外围；边缘
hub	*n.* a center of activity or interest or commerce or transportation; a focal point around which events revolve 中心

Task 1 *Read the article and pick up the best choice.*

1. What is "student mobility" in paragraph 1?

    A) It refers to students who possesses money to study abroad.

    B) It refers to students migrating across borders for higher education.

    C) It refers to students who want to study in another country.

    D) It refers to students whose parents are migrants.

2. What have students realized about studying abroad?

    A) It can open their horizon.

    B) It can help them study more effectively.

    C) It can facilitate their independence.

    D) It can increase their career options.

3. Which of the following is NOT the new mode of education?

    A) Cake Programs.

    B) Distance learning.

    C) Branch campuses.

    D) Joint and dual degrees.

4. What is the general trend of student mobility?

    A) Flow from Asian countries to European countries.

    B) Flow from economically less developed toward economically developed countries.

    C) Flow from regional cities to international cities.

    D) Flow from the West to the East.

Task 2 *Please share ideas with your partners about the following questions based on what you read.*

1. Why do most countries like to have more overseas students?

2. Can you list the factors which influence students' flow in studying abroad?

3. Why should Asian universities engage internationally?

Task 3 *Please retell the following short paragraph by using your own words.*

According to UNESCO data, 165 million students participated in formal tertiary education worldwide in 2009; this is an increase of 65 million students since 2000 and a growth of 65 %. The number of foreign students increased during the same period, from 2.1 to 3.7 million students, which is a growth of 77 %. Consequently, the proportion of foreign students among all tertiary students grew by 7 % from 2000 to 2009.

Task 4 *Please make a survey among your peers and report the result of your survey in class. You are recommended to do the survey with your group members. The following questions may be included in your survey.*

1. Why do/don't they want to study abroad?
2. What are the advantages and disadvantages of studying abroad?
3. What should they do to prepare for studying abroad?
4. Will they plan to go back to China if graduating from universities abroad and explain why?
5. How should we do to continue global communication and cooperation during the spread of COVID-19 pandemic?

Part Four   Speaking after Listening

IELTS Speaking Skill — Expressing Opinion

It is very common that one needs to express opinion about questions asked or some specific topics given. You can use the following expressions when expressing your idea.

From my point of view,
From my perspective,
I believe ...
In my view,
It seems to me that ...
I would say ...

But if you want to make your own statement stronger, you can do it by adding an adverb or adjective as follows.

I *really* think ...
I *strongly* believe ...
I *truly* feel ...
In my *honest* opinion, ...

Task 1   *The following items contain important vocabulary from the lecture "Higher Education in Great Britain". Work with a partner and match vocabulary terms with their definitions. Check your answers in a dictionary if necessary.*

_____ 1. They come from a range of backgrounds and have **varying** expectations of what their study in the country will be like ...

_____ 2. ... a total of nearly 276,350 students attending full-time courses in **establishments** of further education, ...

_____ 3. University first degree courses in arts and sciences are normally of three or four years' **duration** and, ...

_____ 4. ... students are **admitted** for any shorter period of study.

_____ 5. ...a first **diploma** course of more than one-year's duration must apply.

_____ 6. The UCCA will continue to send application forms to universities for consideration at their **discretion** for a limited period after 15 December.

_____ 7. ... these candidates' application forms are again sent to those universities which still have **vacancies**.

_____ 8. It is very rare for a student who has begun a first degree course at one university in Britain to **transfer** to another British university.

_____ 9. ... there is no **provision** for the automatic granting of "credit" for university studies already undertaken.

_____ 10. Students who have already completed some university level study should make **enquiries** directly with the individual university.

a. an instance of questioning

b. move from one place to another

c. marked by diversity or difference

d. a document which may be awarded to a student who has completed a course of study by a university or college

e. an organization founded and united for a specific purpose

f. allow to enter; grant entry to

g. a stipulated condition

h. being unoccupied

i. the period of time during which something continues

j. the power of making free choices unconstrained by external agencies

Task 2 *Listen to a talk about "Higher Education in Great Brain", and choose the best answer according to have you have heard.*

1. How can student get the information about courses and entrance requirements?

A) The school will provide.

B) The teachers will provide.

C) Write directly to the university.

D) Ask for former schoolmates.

2. How many terms are there in one academic year?

A) Two.   B) Three.

C) Four.   D) Five.

3. What is the function of UCCA?

A) Dealing with application for admission.

B) Printing handbooks for application.

C) Branch campuses.

D) Joint and dual degrees.

4. Why are there some candidates put into the "Clearing House Scheme"?

A) Because they fail in entrance exams.

B) Because there is no vacancy in their targeted majors.

C) Because they fail to obtain a place in the initial selection period.

D) Because they want to change their major in universities.

5. Which of the following is correct about transfer in the UK?

A) It is very rare for students to transfer.

B) It is not easy for art students to transfer.

C) The credits can be granted partially by the university you transfer to.

D) The credits cannot be granted by the university you transfer to.

6. Which of the following is correct about admission in the UK?

A) It is a must to have three passes at advanced level.

B) There is an option for students about the GCE test.

C) It is of no use for the candidates having certificates in their own country.

D) High score in GCE test will ensure their admission.

Task 3 *Please paraphrase the following sentence by using your own words.*

In 1973 to 1974 there were over 251,200 full-time students in universities, of whom almost 10% were from overseas, a total of nearly 276,350 students attending full-time courses in establishments of further education, and about 130,270 in colleges of education.

Task 4 *Please discuss with your partners about the following questions. Try to use expressions of showing opinion discussed in the previous part. You can do peer or self-evaluation by using the criteria below.*

1. Why do you think people choose to study in the UK?

2. How do you think of the policy that credits gotten in previous universities cannot be calculated by the universities you want to transfer to?

3. How do you comment on the policy that the grades gotten in Gaokao can be used to apply for programs in British universities?

Criteria for Peer- / Self-Assessment

NO.	Analytic Items	Proportion	Peer- /Self-Assessment
1	Using the expressions of expressing opinion properly	20%	
2	Fluency (less accidental pauses, short pause length, less self-correction)	20%	
3	Accuracy (accuracy in using words and expressions, accuracy in grammar use)	20%	
4	Complexity(lexical variety, usage of less frequent vocabulary, syntactic complexity)	20%	
5	Pronunciation (no strong accent, correct stress, liaison, plosion in words and sentences, sounds naturally)	20%	
Total Score (use a 10-point scale)			

Education, Training and Learning Aspects in Confucianism

The function of education, training and learning is regarded in Confucianism as one of the most important elements for human beings. The concept of Confucianism originates from the founder's name of Kung Fu Tzu (Master Kung) or Confucius (551—479 BCE). He was born in the state of Lu of an aristocratic family. He was studious throughout his lifetime, and, according to history, he achieved a top political position in his native state. Confucius was highly respected and was also considered to be a great educator in his time. Because of his emphasis on the importance of education, Confucius was regarded as one of the first educators in the world.

He had maintained a school with a large number of disciples (over 3,000) for the elucidation of knowledge and wisdom. Confucius believed that only highly educated people, who possess wisdom and profound knowledge, should take leading positions in all areas of society, because their impacts on a broad society are so huge. Confucius believed that a superior culture and civilization could be established through education. Although his philosophical and educational thinking was not widespread or well accepted in his own time, the impact of his thinking became one of the most important social and cultural factors until today, not only in China, but also other East Asian countries in particular Korea and Japan. The various aspects of the Confucian teaching concerning the correct attitudes of education and learning have been studied, interpreted, analyzed and selected from the Confucian classics and shown below in different categorizes.

Self-motivation, self-respect and joy in learning

Concerning the importance of education and learning, Confucius argued that people could not learn unless they were eager to learn. He said that the teacher or master should teach only people, who really want to learn. According to Confucius, it is possible to know whether a person is eager to learn or not, for example, by telling some case stories. If the person can immediately respond by making some analogous inferences related to the case stories, the person is a good learner who also has the will and desires to learn. Besides the importance of self-motivation, self-respect has also been recognized and emphasized to be a critical factor in learning. According to Confucian teaching, whoever mistreats him/herself is not worthy to be advised, and whoever throws him/herself away cannot be helped. In a Confucian context, persons who disregard order and justice in their own words and behaviors are mistreating and cheating themselves. According to Confucius, people can find a teacher everywhere, if a person is self-motivated to learn: "If there are just three people gathered there is a teacher."

Continuous learning

Another message of Confucius concerning education and learning is the emphasis on the importance of continuous learning through one's whole lifetime. He was especially conscious of the difficulty in maintaining existing knowledge or knowledge one has already attained. The ideal way of learning according to Confucius is "... to attain new knowledge every day, and to maintain knowledge achieved before." Thus, one should study hard and in a hurry as if he/she does not have enough time to learn, and at the same time, one should be afraid as if the achieved knowledge is disappearing. He was keenly aware that previously achieved knowledge could easily disappear if the person does not take care of them through endless repetition and practice this knowledge.

Interaction between learning, thinking and reflection

Confucius also stated that it is important to combine the function of learning and the function of thinking or reflection. Ideal learning is a combination of learning and the thinking/reflection processes. In his own words: "Study without thinking/reflection is a waste of time, thinking without study is dangerous."

While Confucius recommended and emphasized the importance of the combination of study and reflection, he warned of the uselessness of a one-sided focus, and he warned especially of the uselessness of thinking which is not preceded by study. Thus, the function of thinking in a Confucian context seems to be recognized as important only when thinking is connected to the studied material. At the same time, he also warned of the uselessness of study that is not combined with thinking and reflection. While he warned about the uselessness of thinking without study, he recommended personal reflection in general. According to Analects, Confucius reflected every day by asking himself whether or not he had failed to repeat and practice what he had learned: ... I examine and reflect on myself concerning these three points: in acting on behalf of others, have I always been loyal to their interests? In my relationship with my friends, have I always been trustworthy to my word? And have I failed to repeat and practice what I have been taught?

Having a good teacher and a good atmosphere

Self-motivation is important for learning, however, having a good teacher and a good atmosphere is also important. In this Confucian context, the meaning of teacher is not a person whose job is to teach. All learned men who have a deeper knowledge than one's self, are regarded as a teacher. Confucius said that if just three persons are gathered, we could find a teacher who has something to teach us. Thus, both Confucius and Hsun Tzu (another great philosopher within the Confucian School) emphasized how critical a factor it is to keep a close relationship to those who are learned and who have a better character than one's own. Confucius warned that people should not form any personal relationships with others if they possess an inferior character, because they can influence you. In learning, nothing is more beneficial than to keep close to those who are learned, and of the roads to learning, none is quicker than to love such men.

Task 1   *Read the article and introduce Confucius to your partners by using your own words. You can refer to the information in the article and your prior knowledge. You can refer to the following points.*

1. Birthplace

2. Personality

3. Contribution

4. ...

Task 2 *Please illustrate the main advocacy of Confucius about education. Give details for each main point and fill the form below.*

1	Self-motivation, self-respect and joy in learning	
2	Continuous learning	
3	Interaction between learning, thinking and reflection	
4	Having a good teacher and a good atmosphere	

Task 3 *Tell your partner which advocacy of Confucius you agree most and explain why.*

1. The point I agree to most
2. The reason

Task 4 *Listen to a lecture about "Learning and Education of John Dewey" and fill the following sentences according to what you hear.*

1. John Dewey is one of the well-known American _____ and educational theorists, who probably have made the most significant contribution to the development of _____ in modern time.

2. After a two-year engagement as a high school teacher, he continued to study philosophy and since _____ in 1884, from John Hopkins University, he went on to a number of _____ at various universities.

3. As a philosopher, he _____ Charles Peirce (1839 — 1914) and William James

(1842 — 1910), who were the _____ of early American _____.

4. As an education theorist, he is particularly well known for his experience and experimental based learning theory including the idea of the _____ between thinking and reflection in learning, the unity between body and mind in learning, the influence of _____ in learning as well as his advocacy for _____ in education.

Task 5 *Listen to the lecture again and choose the best answer according to what you hear.*

1. Which of the following is true about John Dewey?

    A) He is a famous British philosopher and psychologist.

    B) He contributes greatly to the development of educational thinking.

    C) He had been a high-school teacher for three years.

    D) He got his doctor degree from Harvard University.

2. Which of the following is one of the most important factors when considering the issues of learning and knowledge development?

    A) The interaction between the human organism and its environment.

    B) The interaction between thinking and reflection.

    C) The unity between body and mind.

    D) The unity between theory and action.

3. What is the central concept in Dewey's thinking on learning and education?

    A) Behavior.

    B) Perception.

    C) Cognition.

    D) Experience.

4. Which of the following is the correct learning process according to Dewey's theory of inquiry?

    A) practice — inquiry of why — problem awareness — reflection and building a mental master-plan — checking and implementation of the new practice — testing the hypothesis

    B) problem awareness — practice — inquiry of why — testing the hypothesis — reflection and building a mental master-plan checking and implementation of the new practice

    C) practice — problem awareness — inquiry of why — reflection and building a mental master-plan — testing the hypothesis — checking and implementation of the new practice

D) practice — problem awareness — reflection and building a mental master-plan inquiry of why — checking and implementation of the new practice — testing the hypothesis

5. What are the two dimensions of Dewey's leaning model?

   A) the body level and the physical level

   B) the intellectual level and the physical level

   C) the intellectual level and the mind level

   D) the cognitive level and the behavioral level

Task 6　*Please compare ideas about education between Confucius and John Dewey. Can you list the differences and similarities?*

Similarities	Differences

Task 7　*Please share your idea with your partners about one of the following statements.*

1. One's success depends more on nurture rather than nature.

2. If we teach today's students as we taught yesterday's, we rob them of tomorrow.

3. The roots of education are bitter, but the fruit is sweet.

4. A teacher affects eternity; he can never tell where his influence stops.

5. Education is the ability to listen to almost anything without losing your temper or your self-confidence.

6. From the very beginning of his education, the child should experience the joy of discovery.

Words and Expressions about Education

education 教育
educational background 教育程度
educational history 学历
curriculum 课程
major 主修
minor 辅修
educational highlights 课程重点部分
curriculum included 课程包括
specialized courses 专业课程
courses taken 所学课程
courses completed 已修完的课程
rewards 奖励
scholarship 奖学金
"Three Goods" student 三好学生
excellent League member 优秀团员
excellent leader 优秀干部
student council 学生会
off-job training 脱产培训
in-job training 在职培训
educational system 学制
academic year 学年
semester 学期（美）
term 学期（英）
president 校长
vice-president 副校长
dean 院长
academic dean 教务长
academic chairman 系主任
professor 教授
associate professor 副教授
guest professor 客座教授

lecturer 讲师
teaching assistant 助教
research fellow 研究员
research assistant 助教研究员
supervisor 论文导师
principal 中学校长（美）
headmaster 中学校长（英）
master 小学校长（美）
dean of studies 教务长
dean of students 教导主任
probation teacher 代课教师
tutor 导师
governess 女家庭教师
intelligence quotient (IQ) 智商
pass 及格
fail 不及格
auditor 旁听生
government-supported student 公费生
commoner day student 走读生
intern 实习生
prize fellow 奖学金生
boarder 寄宿生
classmate 同班同学
schoolmate 同校同学
graduate 毕业生
scholar 学者
Philosophy 哲学
Philosophy of Marxism 马克思主义哲学
Chinese Philosophy 中国哲学
Foreign Philosophy 外国哲学
Logic 逻辑学

Ethics 伦理学

Aesthetics 美学

Economics 经济学

Theoretical Economics 理论经济学

Political Economics 政治经济学

History of Economics 经济史

Western Economics 西方经济学

World Economics 世界经济学

Population, Resources and Environmental Economics 人口资源和环境经济学

Applied Economics 应用经济学

International Trade 国际贸易

Labor Economics 劳动经济学

Statistics 统计学

Science of Law 法学

Jurisprudence 法学理论

Legal History 法律史

Constitutional Law and Administrative Law 宪法学与行政法学

Criminal Jurisprudence 刑法学

Science of Procedure Laws 诉讼法学

Science of Economic Law 经济法学

Science of Environment and Natural Resources Protection Law 环境与资源保护法学

Political Science 政治学

Political Theory 政治学理论

International Relations 国际关系学

Diplomacy 外交学

Sociology 社会学

Demography 人口学

Anthropology 人类学

Folklore (including Chinese Folk Literature) 民俗学（含中国民间文学）

Ethnology 民族学

Education 教育学

Educational Principle 教育学原理

Curriculum and Teaching Methodology 课程与教学论

History of Education 教育史

Comparative Education 比较教育学

Pre-school Education 学前教育学

Higher Education 高等教育学

Adult Education 成人教育学

Vocational and Technical Education 职业技术教育学

Special Education 特殊教育学

Education Technology 教育技术学

Psychology 心理学

Basic Psychology 基础心理学

Developmental and Educational Psychology 发展教育心理学

Applied Psychology 应用心理学

Science of Physical Culture and Sports 体育学

special training 特别训练

social practice 社会实践

part-time jobs 业余工作

summer jobs 暑期工作

vacation jobs 假期工作

refresher courses 进修课程

extracurricular activities 课外活动

physical activities 体育活动

recreational activities 娱乐活动

academic activities 学术活动

social activities 社会活动

marks 分数

grades 分数

scores 分数

examination 考试

grade 年级

class 班级

monitor 班长

vice-monitor 副班长

commissary in charge of studies 学习委员

commissary in charge of entertainment 文娱委员

commissary in charge of sports 体育委员

commissary in charge of physical labor 劳动委员

Party branch secretary 党支部书记

League branch secretary 团支部书记

Commissary in charge of organization 组织委员

Commissary in charge of publicity 宣传委员

degree 学位

post doctorate 博士后

doctor (Ph. D) 博士

abroad student 留学生

returned student 回国留学生

undergraduate 本科生

senior 大学四年级学生；高中三年级学生

junior 大学三年级学生；高中二年级学生

sophomore 大学二年级学生；高中一年级学生

freshman 大学一年级学生

guest student 旁听生（英）

IELTS Speaking Skill — PPF Strategy

PPF strategy is a kind of approach one can adopt in speaking with the logic as illustrated in the following chart. By using the "PPF Strategy", the speaker actually organize his speech in a chronologic order or time order. First, the speaker should describe what was happened in the past, then what is now followed by the future prediction.

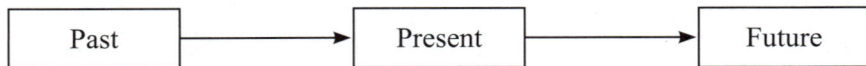

$$\boxed{\text{Past}} \longrightarrow \boxed{\text{Present}} \longrightarrow \boxed{\text{Future}}$$

Task 1   *Please tell your partner why you want to study abroad by using PPF Strategy. You can refer to the following outline.*

When I was young/ a child, ...

Now I am a college student majoring in ..., ...

In the future, I will ... after graduating from ...

Task 2   *Please tell your partner why you like to read one type of book by using PPF Strategy. You can refer to the following outline.*

When I was a little boy, I was told by ... that ...

As a freshman in … University where there is a huge library, …

I believe when I start my career in the future, I will …

IELTS Speaking Test Items

Part 1

1. What was the first school you attended?

2. Do you like your high school?

3. Why did you choose this university?

4. Do you like your professors and classmates? Why?

5. Do you prefer to study in the morning or in the afternoon? Why?

6. What subject do you like or dislike?

7. What was your feeling about the first day you were to school/college?

8. Where do you prefer to study?

9 .What do you do during the process of long-time learning?

10. Why do you choose the current major?

▶ **Sample Answer**

1. What was the first school you attended?

   Well, the first school I attended is called "Anquan Ba" elementary school, which was located in a small village of Sichuan Province. I really enjoyed studying there although the school was poorly equipped and the classroom was shabby. Quite a lot of fun I got there cannot be obtained when I studied in city schools afterwards.

9. What do you do during the process of long-time learning?

   Actually, I suffered from cervical pain because I used to work for a long time without proper rest. So I developed a habit of stretching myself and doing self-massage at regular intervals during the process of long-time learning or work. Otherwise, the pain will be even worse, which hinders my further work or study. Besides, I always look far into the distance to relieve my eye tiredness.

Part 2

1. Describe a skill that you think you can teach other people.

You should say:

What it is;

When you learned it;

How you can teach others;

And how you feel about this skill.

▶ **Sample Answer**

A skill that I acquired recently and would be pleased to be able to impart to others is baking. Stuck at home amid the pandemic, with plenty of spare time on my hands. I tried to do something worthwhile.

Things changed on one day in April. I finally got the hang of it after having watched several Youtube videos in a row. Inspired by Christina Tosi and Cupcake Jemma these two creative YouTubers, I bought all the baking instruments out of passion and curiosity. At first, I followed the naked cake recipe, mingled all the ingredients, poured the mixture into the baking model. Just several hours, the liquid mixture gradually bulged out. Fluffy cake is demonstrating my first successful baking experiment. My mom was also tempted by the super-duper flavor and she was so curious about the magic of the oven.

I'm not bragging. Now I can confidently say I'm almost like a pro, of course, a family-style one. Maybe I can start with helping someone else who is rubbish at it just like I was or I might do an online tutorial, just like a Chinese YouTuber. Imagine how amazing it's gonna be. One cool thing is the precise baking process gonna be a lot easier for others. Basically, my friends won't need to always wait for the reopening of the favorite dessert shop anymore. On the contrary, they can do the same yummy dessert on their own.

On top of that, after I post my tutorial video online, I might get more followers which are gonna be nice. Still, there is something I'm slightly worried about too because my home-made tutorial could be viewed by everyone. I might accidentally fail, every tiny mistake may be exaggerated by the public which may embarrass me. But anyway, what I really want is just to share the fun of baking and killing the tedious time. So even just one person follows my baking video but gain the pleasure, I would be strongly satisfying. After all, sharing is loving.

2. Describe a book you read that you find useful
   You should say:
   What the book was;
   When and where you read it;
   What is was about;
   And explain why you find it useful.

3. Describe the first time you used a foreign language to talk to someone
   You should say:
   What language you used;
   When and where it happened;
   What you talked about;
   And explain how you felt about it.

Part 3

1. Should teachers be funny when they teach?
2. What qualities should teachers have?
3. Which do you think is more important, practical skills or academic skills?
4. Which age group is the best at learning new things?

▶ **Sample Answer**
1. Should a teacher be funny in the class?
   Absolutely. I believe that it is helpful if a teacher is humorous at times. First, as for the class itself, a funny teacher could make the atmosphere more enjoyable and vivid. Harsh teachers' classes usually are less attractive than the funny teachers'. What's more, due to the charms of the teachers, the students pay more attention to the subject, even if the course is pretty challenging. From a

psychological aspect, students prefer showing the good studying results before the teacher they like. So it is pretty important for a teacher being funny in the class.

2. What qualities should teachers have?

Well, massive qualities are required for a teacher. First of all, a good teacher must have excellent interpersonal skill to build trusting relationships with students to create a positive and productive learning environment. For instance, a great teacher should always be willing to listen to students when there is a problem. Moreover, a competent teacher must gain and apply knowledge of the cognitive and emotional development of learners. Just like he must understand the pace and capacity of the student. Then I believe an inspired teacher ought to have a love of teaching or passion for the work. Only the teacher contains the love for this profession, he or she will practice the real meaning of education.

3. Which is more important, practical skills or academic skills?

Oh, that's a tricky question. Actually, it's great to have a university degree and develop academic skills like how to spot the research gap, how to analyze data and how to present the research in academic community. We may foster a scientific way of thinking by acquiring academic skills, which is especially important for those who want to further their study after undergraduate study. On the other hand, the practical skill is also necessary in actual working environment, like typing and organizing things, dealing with customers, selling products, etc. Still, in this day and age, some down-to-earth knowledge and abilities are also highly-valued. You see, not everyone can do carpentering or plumbing. I plan to get a master degree abroad, so I value academic skills more than practical skills.

4. Which age group is the best at learning new things?

For me, I reckon the age of young adult is the best at acquiring something fresh. Let me take college students as an example, who undoubtedly belong to young adult. They are full of energy and passion, who are curious about everything around and are eager to probe for the unknown and the uncertain. Besides their memory including working memory and long-term memory is at the peak, which makes it pretty easy for them to memorize and understand new concepts. This is something older adults had difficulty with. Thirdly, college students don't have to undertake so much living burden. They generally don't need to worry about the salaries, the marriage, the educational problems of their children even the medical issue about their parents. I mean they have enough time and energy to focus on studying. Fourthly, young adults are maturer than the teenagers. So they know it is important to learn some new things and they are more self-disciplined than the adolescent. Based on the above reasons, I cling to the idea that young adult is the best age at learning new things.

5. Do you think library will disappear in the future?

6. What can be done to make libraries more popular?

7. What books are interesting to young people?

8. Are there any differences about preferences of young and old people towards books?

9. Do you prefer to speak or read more?

10. Is writing an important skill?

11. Do people write often these days?

12. What is the most effective way to adopt a foreign language?

13. What can hinder a person's learning a foreign language?

Checklist for This Chapter

Please check according to the scale from 1 to 5.

(1 — Strongly Disagree; 2 — Disagree; 3 — Undecided; 4 — Agree; 5 — Strongly Agree)

Can-do List	1	2	3	4	5
I know what IELTS Speaking Test is.					
I can use signpost language in speaking.					
I know how to express my opinion.					
I can use PPF strategy in speaking.					
I know the value of educational theories from Confucius and John Dewey.					
Self-reflection 1. In which part have I done very well? 2. In which part should I make improvement? 3. What should I do to bridge the current gap? 4. What suggestions do I have for my teacher or the class arrangement? 5. Anything I would like to say.					
(Your reflection could be written in Chinese)					

2

Environment

LEARNING OBJECTIVES

In this chapter you will learn

- ■ what IELTS Speaking Test Part 1 is like
- ■ how to give extended answers in IELTS Speaking Test
- ■ how to clarify and confirm ideas
- ■ how to pronounce better
- ■ the notion of green eco-environment consevation in China

Part One   Warming-up

Task 1   *List evidence that you know for global warming. Share ideas with your partners. You may jot down the key words in the following box while preparing for your description.*

1.
2.
3.

Task 2 *Listen to a short talk on "Taoism and Sustainability", then fill the blanks in the following sentences.*

1. Thomas Alexander argues that philosophers in the West have not usually presented satisfactory frameworks for _____.

2. The importance of _____ can be derived from ancient principles of east Asian philosophy — Taoism.

3. Taoism includes following _____ of nature while not hurting other persons.

4. One should behave more _____ and less _____.

5. Taoism is therefore a _____ requiring an understanding of the ever-changing balance between human activity and the environment.

6. One should not pursue a lifestyle that _____ impacts the natural environment.

Task 3 *Please list what Taoism advocates to achieve a mutual balance between human society and nature in terms of your knowledge. You may discuss with your partners and compare your discussion results with other groups.*

NO.	Claims
1	
2	
3	
4	

Part Two   IELTS Speaking Test

General introduction to IELTS Speaking Test Part 1

In Part 1 of the IELTS Speaking Test, the examiner asks you basic questions about yourself and asks to see your identification. Further, the examiner asks you some questions about yourself, your family or home town, your job or studies, and a range of similar topics or areas that you are familiar with. This section lasts for 4 to 5 minutes and you have to give brief answers to display your command over language.

Part 1 goes in the following steps:

Step 1   The examiner asks the candidate to *state his name* and *confirms the candidate's* country of origin.

Step 2   The examiner asks to *see the candidate's identification* (the identification you used to register for the test: ID card or passport).

Step 3   The examiner asks the candidate to *answer questions about home town or occupation*.

Step 4   The examiner asks the candidate to *answer questions about a familiar topic of general interest.* (The examiner may ask several related questions to give the candidate a chance to *extend their answers*)

Possible Types of Questions can be Asked

- your country of origin
- your home town
- how long you have lived there
- what you do: work or study
- your interests and future plans
- family and family relationship
- ...

- modern and traditional life styles
- traditional and modern buildings
- tourism and tourist sites
- celebrations and cultural activities
- schooling and the education system
- city and country living

Abilities Tested

- ability to provide full answers to all questions
- ability to give longer responses to some questions
- ability to give information by describing and explaining

Important to Know

- *Participate fully.* If you do not participate fully in the conversation, you may not achieve the potential band score because you may not have been able to demonstrate the level of language you are capable of producing.
- *Use synonyms* rather than repeating a single word to express the same idea.

- *Do not answer with pre-prepared answers* or you will seem not natural.

- You can *ask the interviewer to repeat* the question if you do not understand it.

- *Answer with a certain logic* (organizational structure) which will help your listeners follow with much ease.

IELTS Speaking Skill — Providing Extended Answers

Participating fully allows your examiner to assess your language ability comprehensively, so it's necessary for you to extend your answer to a proper length. There are several strategies to extend your answers in Part 1 answers. Generally, they are some lexical items that help you provide more details. Please check the following table for them.

Table 2-1   Strategies of IELTS Speaking Test Part 1

Strategies	Description	Sample questions	Sample Answers
Feelings and Opinions	Answer by saying how you feel about the question you were just asked.	*What do you like to do in your spare time?*	*I like shopping because I love trying on new clothes and I always feel more confident when I'm wearing a new outfit.*
Contrasting Details	Use the word "but" to contrast details.	*How long have you worked there?*	*I've worked there for three years, but I'm going to change careers next year.*
Combining Details	Add in some extra details with "and" "with" or "also", etc.	*Do you live in a flat or a house?*	*I live in a house with my two brothers and my mum. We've also got a dog and a cat.*
Past Comparisons	Talk about what you "used to" do and how that has changed now in the present.	*Do you play sport?*	*I used to love basketball, but now I play football more because that's what my friends are into.*
Adding Reasons	Explain why you think or do something in the test. You can do this using "because" or "so".	*Do you like your job?*	*Yes, I really love my job because I get to help people with their problems everyday.*

Strategies	Description	Sample questions	Sample Answers
Future	If something will change in the future, you can use one of the future structures, like "will" or "be + going to".	*Do you work or study?*	*I'm at university at the moment, but I'm graduating next year and I will hopefully get a job in advertising.*
Contrast Opposite Opinions	You might be asked a question where you have to talk about your opinion or another person's opinion. Use "even so" or "although" to show that you have considered both sides.	*Is your home town a nice place for tourists to visit?*	*Yes, it has a really nice beach, although it is getting really busy these days, so it's not as pristine as it used to be.*
Giving Examples	Real life examples are always the easiest things to talk about because you can talk about them naturally and in more detail.	*Do you get along with your brothers?*	*No, we're not into the same things, like when we are both watching TV we always fight about what show to watch.*
Frequency	You can use words like "usually", "never", "always" and "more often than not" to extend your answers.	*What do you do at the weekends?*	*I usually watch TV and play computer games, but sometimes I go out for a drink with my friends.*

Remember, combining two or three of the above structures in a single answer is very impressive. However, trying too hard to use "complex structures" normally leads to mistakes. Remember that the main goal in the Speaking Test is being able to communicate effectively and fluently with the examiner. If you are thinking about complicated grammar structures, you probably won't be able to do either of those things. You do have to use a "range of structures", but that does not mean that you have to use every complicated phrase and tense in the English language. Focus on real communication and the "range of structures" will look after themselves.

Task 1   *It is customary that the examiner will ask your name first. He/she then will ask you to show your identity and want to know what you do, where you are from and some basic conversation-starter questions. Work with your partner to practice answering the following questions in turn.*

- Good morning. My name is Katherin Hingis. Could I have your name, please?
- And your candidate number?
- Can I see your ID?
- Well, great. Where are you from?
- What do you do?

Task 2   *After knowing your basic information, the examiner will ask you some questions that will allow you to give extended answers to show your language ability. Please work with your partner to answer the following questions on the cards. After a round of questions and answers, talk with your partner what strategies you employed to extend your answers.*

Card 1

Do you have many friends?

How often do you go out with friends?

Tell me about your best friend at school.

How friendly are you with your neighbors?

Which is more important to you, friends or family?

Card 2

Did your parents choose your name(s)?

How did your parents choose your name(s)?

Does your name have any special meaning?

Is your name common or unusual in your country?

If you could change your name, would you?

Card 3

How popular are bicycles in your home town?

How often do you ride a bicycle? Why or why not?

Do you think that bicycles are suitable for all ages?

What are the advantages of a bicycle compared to a car?

Card 4

What games are popular in your country?

Do you play any games?

How do people learn to play games in your country?

Do you think it's important for people to play games?

Part Three   Speaking after Reading

How Will Climate Change Affect the World and Society?

Climate change is already affecting the planet and society and will continue to do so for generations to come. The physical and chemical changes of human activities are being felt in natural ecosystems on land and at sea, on farms and ranches, and in cities and suburbs, but the changes are not happening uniformly. Differences in how regions are affected by varying degrees of warming, precipitation, and changes of animal and plant species are likely to get even more extreme as climate change continues.

The poles have already seen the greatest warming, and will continue to warm more rapidly than other areas. Already we're seeing record losses of ice in the Arctic. That melting ice contributes to rising sea levels, affecting the entire planet. In addition, warm water expands, so sea levels will rise as the atmosphere warms. The ocean has risen 4 to 8 inches (10 to 20 centimeters) globally over the last hundred years. As sea level continues to rise, flooding and storm surges will threaten freshwater sources, as well as coastal homes and buildings. Coastal facilities and barrier islands in many parts of the world are gradually submerging, and some low-lying islands have already had to be evacuated, as Australia's *The Age* (July 29, 2009) describes happening in the Carteret Islands of Papua New Guinea.

As climate change causes the ocean to rise, increased atmospheric carbon dioxide is also changing ocean chemistry. When carbon dioxide dissolves in water, it makes water more acidic. Warmer ocean water also contains less oxygen. These changes harm marine ecosystems, destroying coral reefs that shelter much of the ocean's biodiversity, and harming many other species. In addition to the harmful effects on natural ecosystems, this affects fish that people eat, coral reefs that tourists visit, and the whales, dolphins, sharks, and other marine life that fascinate so many people. Climate change and changing oceanic chemistry affect the tiny plankton in the ocean which produce much of the oxygen in our air, as researchers Graeme Hays, Anthony Richardson, and Carol Robinson explained in a 2005 review in Trends in Ecology and Evolution. Changes to the growth of these tiny organisms have surprisingly large effects on global climate, as do climate change-induced changes to the movements of marine life, as reported by *Wired* magazine (July 2009). Changing ocean chemistry thus has complex and unpredictable effects on global climate and even the air we breathe.

The frequency of extreme weather events is increasing through the warming and moistening of the atmosphere. Hot days are becoming even hotter and more frequent, and both drought and heavy rain and snow will continue to occur more often. Because hurricanes draw their strength from the heat of water on the ocean's surface, hurricanes have been getting stronger. Researchers work to understand how these changes to the weather affect coastal populations, not to mention shipping, fishing, and other industries in those waters.

Changes in rainfall and temperature will alter where various plants and animals can live, forcing some species to migrate, disrupting delicate ecosystems, and increasing the rate of extinctions globally. Scientists are studying how different species responded to past climate changes, hoping to better understand the impacts of today's climate change on wildlife. Already, hunters and anglers are seeing changes in migration patterns and animal behavior, and gardeners and farmers see plants sprouting, flowering, and losing their leaves at different times, forcing them to change what they can plant. Historic droughts are forcing farmers to plant different crops, and some farmland is becoming unusable.

As climate change causes plants and animals to relocate, disease will also move, exposing human populations — and crop plants, livestock, and wildlife — to new diseases. Climate change also affects human health and mortality, with the Environmental Protection Agency and the Centers for Disease Control warning about direct effects from rising temperatures, degraded air quality, and greater risks from Lyme disease, hantavirus, and other diseases carried by insects and animals. Drought, degraded air and water quality, and greater hazards in coastal and low-lying regions will, as the World Health Organization points out, create additional health problems, especially among the populations most vulnerable to natural hazards and disease.

As leaders in the U.S. military recognize the effects of climate change will affect the security of nations as conflicts brew over competition for water, food, and land. The prospect of large groups of climate refugees migrating across borders is a concern for governments as well as for organizations devoted to reducing risk and helping those who are living in poverty and in vulnerable regions.

Adapted from the article published on https://ncse.ngo/how-will-climate-change-affect-world-and-society

Word Bank

ecosystem	*n.* all the living things in an area and the way they affect each other and the environment 生态系统
ranch	*n.* a very large farm on which animals are kept, especially in North and South America 农场
uniformly	*adv.* in a way that is the same everywhere or for everyone 一律地；均匀地
precipitation	*n.* water that falls from the clouds towards the ground, especially as rain or snow 降水
surge	*n.* a sudden and great increase 汹涌；波浪，波涛
submerge	*v.* to go below or make something go below the surface of the sea or a river or lake 淹没；把……浸入；沉浸
evacuate	*v.* to move people from a dangerous place to somewhere safe 疏散；撤退
dissolve	*v.* (of a solid) to be absorbed by a liquid, especially when mixed, or (of a liquid) to absorb a solid 使溶解；使分解；使液化
acidic	*adj.* containing acid 酸的，酸性的；产生酸的
coral	*n.* a substance like rock, formed in the sea by groups of particular types of small animal, often used in jewelry 珊瑚
plankton	*n.* very small plants and animals that float on the surface of the sea and on which other sea animals feed 浮游生物（总称）
induce	*v.* to cause something to happen 诱导；引起

moisten	*v.* to make something slightly wet or to become slightly wet 弄湿；使······湿润
migrate	*v.* When an animal migrates, it travels to a different place, usually when the season changes 迁移；移民；移动
angler	*n.* a person whose hobby is trying to catch fish with a rod and line 钓鱼者
sprout	*v.* to produce leaves, hair, or other new developing parts, or (of leaves, hair, and other developing parts) to begin to grow 发芽，萌芽；长出
drought	*n.* a long period when there is little or no rain 干旱，旱灾
mortality	*n.* the number of deaths within a particular society and within a particular period of time 死亡数，死亡率
degrade	*v.* to spoil or destroy the beauty or quality of something 使······降级；使······降低
Lyme disease	*n.* a disease caused by bacteria that are spread by the bite of an insect
Hantavirus	*n.* any one of a group of viruses that are transmitted to humans by rodents and cause disease of varying severity, ranging from a mild form of influenza to respiratory or kidney failure 汉坦病毒
vulnerable	*adj.* able to be easily physically, emotionally, or mentally hurt, influenced, or attack 易受伤害的，脆弱的
brew	*v.* If an unpleasant situation or a storm is brewing, you feel that it is about to happen （暴风雨）酝酿；（危机、困境等）酝酿

Task 1 *Please make a list with your partner about in which aspects climate change may affect the whole world. Support them with details (examples).*

Possible Areas	Supporting Details

Task 2 *Please retell how the world is affected by climate change by summing up this article. You can make use of the above table in your retelling.*

Task 3 *Please make a survey on people's knowledge of climate change. You are recommended to do the survey in your class. The following questions may be included in your survey. Please report the result of your survey in class.*

1. What are the consequences of climate change?
2. How does it change your life?
3. What do you know we common people can do to help it from getting worse?

Part Four   Speaking after Listening

IELTS Speaking Skill — Clarifying and Confirming Points

In the IELTS Speaking Test, it is totally natural not to be able to understand some of the questions the examiner might ask you, and it is totally normal to ask the person you are speaking to for clarification or confirmation if you don't understand.

Remember that even if you are asking for these, you still need to show your manner and demonstrate your ability in language.

There are some expressions you may use to both demonstrate your courtesy and your proficiency.

Sorry, I'm not quite sure I understand what you are saying.

What does ... mean?

If I understand you correctly, ...

Pardon?

Can you speak a little bit more slowly, please?

I'm sorry I didn't quite catch/get that, could you say that again please?

Sorry, could you repeat the question please?

I'm sorry but I don't quite understand ..., can you explain it to me?

I'm a little confused about the ..., can you tell me what it means?

Sorry, can you explain what ... means?

Task 1   *The following items contain important vocabulary from the talk "What is Climate Change". Work with a partner and match vocabulary terms with their definitions. Check your answers in a dictionary if necessary.*

1. antarctica

2. annual

3. precipitation

4. humidity

5. scale

6. fahrenheit

7. orbit

8. volcanic

9. eruption

10. heat-trapping gas

11. carbon dioxide

12. drought

13. hurricane

14. atmosphere

15. unavoidable

a. (of) a measurement of temperature on a standard in which 32° is the temperature at which water freezes and 212° that at which it boils

b. unable to be prevented or stayed away from

c. the gas formed when carbon is burned, or when people or animals breathe out

d. happening once every year

e. a violent wind that has a circular movement, especially in the West Atlantic Ocean

f. water that falls from the clouds towards the ground, especially as rain or snow

g. the continent around the South Pole

h. a long period when there is little or no rain

i. a set of numbers, amounts, etc., used to measure or compare the level of something

j. a measurement of how much water there is in the air

k. of, relating to, or made by a volcano (= a mountain with a hole at the top through which hot liquid rock is or has been forced out)

l. an occasion when a volcano explodes, and flames and rocks come out of it; (of a volcano) the act of doing this

m. the mixture of gases around the earth

n. the curved path through which objects in space move around a planet or star

o. gases that cause Greenhouse effects

Task 2   *Listen to a talk about "What Is Climate Change?", and choose the best answer according to what you have heard.*

1. Which of the following is an improper description of climate of a region?
   A) The climate of Hawaii is warm.
   B) The climate of Antarctic is cold.
   C) The annual rainfall of a region is one element of the climate of a region.
   D) The temperature of February 10, 2020 of Hawaii is one element of the climate there.

2. Which of the following is an improper statement of weather of a region?
   A) Weather changes every day.
   B) The weather of Hawaii tomorrow is sunny.
   C) The weather of a region or city may tend to be warm and humid during summer.
   D) Weather is the short-term changes we see in temperature.

3. According to most scientist, what contribute to the recent warming in climate?
   A) Changes of the Earth's orbit.
   B) Burning of coal, gas and oil.
   C) Volcanic eruption.
   D) All of above.

4. According to the talk, what is not one of the impacts of climate change?
   A) Melting snow and ice and further rising sea levels.
   B) Hotter waves and stronger hurricanes.
   C) Vegetation patterns are changing.
   D) Rainfall patterns are changing.

5. What can individuals do to prevent the climate from warming up?
   A) Make use of sun, wind and water energies.
   B) Save water and energy.
   C) Get ready for land loss caused by rising sea level.
   D) Limit the emission of greenhouse gases.

Task 3   *Listen again and take notes by following the outline in the box.*

What is climate?

What is weather?

What is the difference between weather and climate?

What are the possible causes of climate change?

What are the possible impacts of climate change?

What have been done?

What can average people do?

Task 4   *Please compare your notes with your partners. Try to use expressions of clarification and confirmation discussed in the previous part to check how much information you share with each other or disagree with each other. While you are doing the conversation, you could evaluate each other's language use by using the criteria in the following table.*

Criteria for Peer- / Self-Assessment

NO.	Analytic Items	Proportion	Peer- /Self-Assessment
1	Basic 4 standards (Fluency, accuracy, complexity, ronunciation)	40%	
2	Use of expressions of clarification where necessary	20%	
3	Use of expressions of confirmation where necessary	20%	
4	Use of polite language	20%	
Total Score (use a 10-point scale)			

Usher in a New Era of Ecological Progress

Our efforts for ecological conservation and environmental protection will benefit future generations. We must be aware that it is a pressing and difficult task to protect the environment and control pollution, and that it is important and necessary to advance ecological progress. We must take a responsible attitude towards our people and future generations, be resolute in controlling environmental pollution, strive to usher in a new era of ecological progress and improve the environment for our people to live and work in.

Ecological progress is of vital importance to the future of the nation and the wellbeing of its people. The 18th National Congress of the CPC listed ecological progress along with economic, political, cultural and social progress as the five goals in the overall plan for the cause of Chinese socialism, vowing to promote ecological progress to build a beautiful China and achieve lasting and sustainable development of the Chinese nation.

To promote ecological progress, we must comprehensively implement the guiding principles of the Party's 18th National Congress, and take Deng Xiaoping Theory, the important thought of the Three Represents and the Scientific Outlook on Development as our guide. We must raise awareness of the need to respect, protect, and accommodate ourselves to nature, follow the basic state policy of resource conservation and environmental protection, and give high priority to conserving resources, protecting the environment and promoting its natural restoration. We must dedicate ourselves to raising our ecological awareness, enhancing relevant systems, safeguarding ecological security, and improving the environment. We must preserve our geographical space and streamline our industrial structure, our mode of production, and our way of life in the interest of resource conservation and environmental protection.

We must strike a balance between economic growth and environmental protection, and bear in mind that protecting the environment equates to protecting productivity and that improving the environment also equates to developing productivity. We will be more conscientious in promoting green, circular, and low-carbon development. We will never again seek economic growth at the cost of the environment.

It is through land use that ecological progress can be advanced. Maintaining a balance between population, resources and the environment, and promoting economic, social and ecological efficiency, we will determine an overall plan for developing our land, and allot space to production, to daily life, and to ecological development as appropriate, in order to leave more space for nature's self-restoration. We will accelerate the work of functional zoning, follow the functional definitions of different areas where development must be optimized, prioritized, restricted, or forbidden, and delimit and strictly enforce ecological red lines. We will work out appropriate plans for urbanization, agricultural development and ecological security to safeguard national and regional ecological security, and improve services for ecological conservation. We must fully understand the importance of enforcing ecological red lines. Any violations regarding environmental protection will be punished.

Resource conservation is a fundamental way to protect the environment. We will conserve resources and use them efficiently, bring about a fundamental change in the way resources are utilized, increase conservation efforts in all respects, and drastically reduce the consumption of energy, water and land resources per unit of GDP. We will vigorously develop a circular economy to reduce waste and resource consumption, re-use resources, and recycle waste in the process of production, distribution and consumption.

We will launch major projects to restore the ecosystem, and increase our capacity for producing eco-friendly products. A sound ecological environment is the basic foundation for the sustainable development of humanity and society. The public are greatly concerned about the environment. So we should place emphasis on serious environmental problems that pose health hazards to the people, and take a holistic approach to intensifying the prevention and control of water, air and soil pollution, with the focus on water pollution in key river basins and regions, and on air pollution in key industrial sectors and areas.

We must have the strictest possible institutions and legislation in place in order to guarantee ecological progress. To do this, we should first of all improve the evaluation norms for economic and social development to include resource consumption, environmental damage, ecological benefits and other indicators that can be used to assess ecological improvement, and use them to direct and shape our ecological work. We will establish an accountability system, and call to account officials whose ill-judged decisions have caused serious ecological damage.

We will increase publicity and education on the need to promote ecological progress, raise public awareness of the need to conserve resources and protect the environment, and foster a social atmosphere of cherishing our environment.

Xi Jinping，*The Governance of China*, from http://en.qstheory.cn/2020-12/11/c_607614.htm

Task 1   *Read the article and summarize the general ecological thoughts of present Chinese Government to your partners by using your own words. You can refer to the information in the article. You may jot down the key points in the following box.*

Task 2   *In the warming-up section, there was a very brief introduction of the Taoist philosophy of human-nature relationship. Please try to compare the thoughts in this speech and the thoughts in Taoist philosophy, and discuss in a small group about the similarities.*

Task 3   *In President Xi's speech, many aspects of environmental protection have been mentioned. Pick up any one that you are familiar with to give a 1–2 minutes talk. You may have 3 minutes to improve your thought on that, and try to extend the point you've chosen by using the strategies of "extending idea" in Part Two of this unit. You may note down your outline of your talk in the following box.*

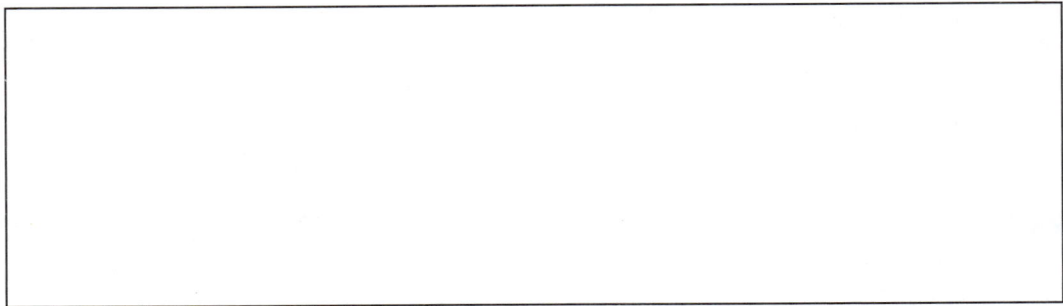

06

Task 4 *Listen to a talk about "climate change has worsened global economic inequality" and fill the following sentences according to what you hear.*

1. Although _____ between countries has decreased in recent decades, the research suggests the gap would have narrowed faster without global warming.

2. The study builds on previous research in which Burke and co-authors analyzed 50 years of annual temperature and GDP measurements for 165 countries to estimate the effects of temperature _____ on economic growth.

3. They demonstrated that growth during warmer than average years has _____ in cool nations and slowed in warm nations.

4. The historical data clearly show that crops are more _____, people are healthier and we are more productive at work when temperatures are neither too hot nor too cold.

5. _____ countries, in particular, tend to have temperatures far outside the ideal for economic growth.

Task 5 *Listen to the talk again and choose the best answer according to what you have heard.*

1. What is the study mentioned in this talk mainly about?

   A) Climate change has a bad impact on the world's economy in a short term.

   B) Climate change has a good impact on the world's economy in a short term.

   C) Climate change has contributed to the economic equality.

   D) Climate change has worsened the economic inequality.

2. "Although economic inequality between countries has decreased in recent decades, the research suggests the gap would have narrowed faster without global warming." According to this sentence, which of the followings is Not true?

   A) The situation of economic inequality between countries is getting better in recent decades.

B) The situation of economic inequality between countries is getting worse in recent decades.

C) If it were not the global warming, the economic gap can be even smaller.

D) If it were not the global warming, the economic gap can be eliminated.

3. The historical data clearly shows the following, except for: _____

A) Temperatures neither too hot and too cold make the crops more productive.

B) Temperatures neither too hot and too cold make people healthier.

C) Temperatures neither too hot and too cold make people more productive at work.

D) Temperatures neither too hot and too cold make unequal economy.

4. Which of the following countries is not near the perfect temperature for economic output according to the speaker?

A) China

B) India

C) Japan

D) United States

5. What is essentially new about this research?

A) This research is a measure of the price for economic products.

B) This research is a new argument for negotiation.

C) This research is an accounting of how much each country has been impacted by global warming.

D) This research is a new explanation of how climate has changed over decades.

Task 6 *Please discuss in a small group about climate change. Tell each other whether you believe in climate change and illustrate your idea with supporting details. Jot down important points or vocabularies that might be useful in your talk.*

Words and Expressions about Environment

environment 环境

environmental 有关环境的

environmentalist 环保主义者

environmentally-friendly 保护环境的

natural environment 自然环境

environmental hazard 环境风险

environmental disaster 环境灾难

conservation 保护

conservation program 保护项目

wildlife conservation 野生动植物保护

energy conservation 能源保护

wildlife 野生动植物

local wildlife 本地野生生物

native wildlife 本地野生生物

creature 生物

fauna 动物群

flora 植物群

vegetation 植被，植物

species 种类，物种

endangered species 濒危物种

threatened species 受威胁物种，濒危物
    种

rare species 稀有物种

protected species 受保护物种

extinct species 灭绝物种

ecosystem 生态系统

delicately balanced ecosystem 微妙的生
    态系统平衡

fragile ecosystem 脆弱的生态系统

Mother Nature 大自然

diverse 多种多样的

biodiversity 生物多样性

loss of biodiversity 生物多样性缺失

variety of species 各种各样的生物

ecology 生态学

habitat 栖息地

inhabit 栖息，居住

natural surroundings 自然环境

adapt 适应

evolve 演化，演变

evolution 演变，进化

thrive 繁荣，兴旺

marine 海洋的

nocturnal 夜间的

migrate 移动、移居

extinction 灭绝

dying out 灭绝

climate 气候

climate change 气候变化

combat climate change 应对气候变化

natural resources 自然资源

rich in natural resources 自然资源丰富

fossil fuels 化石燃料

atmosphere 大气层

ozone layer 臭氧层

carbon dioxide 二氧化碳

carbon monoxide 一氧化碳

greenhouse gas 温室气体

greenhouse effect 温室效应

erosion 侵蚀，腐蚀

coastal erosion 海岸侵蚀

soil erosion 水土流失，土壤侵蚀

wind erosion 风蚀

deforestation 森林开发，乱砍滥伐

land clearance 开荒

logging 采伐（森林）

pollution 污染

pollute 污染

emissions （气体）排放

carbon footprint 碳足迹、碳排放量

global warming 全球变暖

fight / combat / tackle global warming 对抗全球变暖

disposable products 一次性产品

dumping ground 垃圾倾倒场

acid rain 酸雨

contaminate 污染

degradation 退化

depletion 消耗，损耗

fumes 废气

smog 烟雾

air quality 空气质量

poisonous 有毒的

toxic 有毒的

threat 威胁

endanger 危害

poaching 非法猎取

drought 干旱

flooding 洪水

flash floods 山洪

protect 保护

preserve 维持，保护

biodegradable 可生物降解的

carbon-neutral 碳中和，碳平衡

sustainable 可持续的

sustainability 可持续性

renewable energy 可再生能源

solar power 太阳能

energy-efficient 节能的

wind turbine 风力涡轮机

wind farm 风力农场

clean energy 清洁能源

organic farming 有机农业

afforestation 植树造林

go green 变绿，变环保

on foot 步行

safeguard 保护，保护措施

urban 城市的

rural 农村的

IELTS Speaking Skill — Criteria for Pronunciation

To get a good score for pronunciation, it's important to be familiar with the different features of pronunciation that are assessed in the IELTS Speaking Test. Below is a summary of all the different features you'll need to be aware of and practice!

Individual sound accuracy

This is often related to your use of individual sounds. For Chinese students, it's important to pay special attention to some sounds that do not exist in our native language.

Examples

"th", "v", voiced "s"; /i/ v.s. /i:/; ...

Word stress

This means placing the stress or emphasis on the correct syllable in a word. Your use of word stress can affect how easy you are to understand.

Examples

ˈrecord v.s. reˈcord; Com-PU-ter

Sentence stress

This involves the individual word or words in a sentence that you choose to emphasize. It's different from word stress in that it's used to convey meaning.

Examples

"How do you usually go to school?"

"I go to school by subway everyday."

She called you yesterday.

Weak sounds

English words contain a lot of weak syllable sounds, (represented by the phonetic symbol called the 'schwa' /ə/). Knowing which syllables in a word have these sounds can make your English pronunciation sound more natural.

Examples

/ə/ in "about", /æt/ in "at"

I go to school by subway everyday.

Intonation/pitch

Intonation describes the way in which our voice rises and falls when we speak. In IELTS, you raise your intonation when you ask for repetition and clarification; or when you are trying to list items when giving examples.

Examples

Could you say that again put your question another way? ↗

I eat different types of vegetable to keep healthy, such as eggplant ↗, cucumber ↗, celery↗ and so on.

Chunking

Speakers divide speech into "chunks", which may be single words or groups of words to communicate a thought or idea, or to focus on information the speaker thinks is important.

Examples

My parents and I || went to ||see a film || yesterday.

Linking

Native speakers join or "link" words to each other. Because of this linking, the words in a sentence do not always sound the same as when we say them individually. Using linking in pronunciation makes others easy to understand you.

Examples

My father and I went to Beijing last Tuesday.

We all like him because he often tells us some jokes to entertain us.

Task 1　*Read the following sentences with correct pronunciation and stress and please pay special attention to the words in boldface.*

■ She handed the lady a rectangular **object** made of metal.

■ They **object** to his constant lateness.

■ She handed him a beautifully wrapped **present**.

■ She was **presented** with the Oscar.

■ They started work on the research **project** immediately.

■ She always **projects** herself with confidence.

Task 2　*Read the following paragraph and mark the possible pronunciation features mentioned above. You may discuss it with your partner.*

The climate of a region or city is its typical or average weather. For example, the climate of Hawaii is sunny and warm. But the climate of Antarctica is freezing cold. Earth's climate is the average of all the world's regional climates. Climate change, therefore, is a change in the typical or average weather of a region or city. This could be a change in a region's average annual rainfall, for example. Or it could be a change in a city's average temperature for a given month or season.

Climate change is also a change in Earth's overall climate. This could be a change in Earth's average temperature, or a change in Earth's typical precipitation patterns.

IELTS Speaking Test Items

Part 1

1. What can you recycle?
2. How is garbage collected in your neighborhood?
3. Do you waste energy?
4. What types of pollution are there in your city?
5. Do you often take public transportation?
6. What do you do to protect environment?
7. Does your country often suffer from natural disaster? Which one?
8. Are you educated about protecting the environment at school?

▶ **Sample Answer**

4. What types of pollution are there in your city?

The first one came to my mind is noise pollution. You see, in big cities, it is just a fact of life that you live with. In my home town, it is the same. Almost every household owns a car which means more cars would be jammed on the road; more construction sites get popped up because the metros are under construction. The noise pollution was getting worse in recent years. I hope this situation will get better in the future.

6. What do you do to protect environment?

Well, there are a lot of things I can do to contribute my part for environment protection. The most common one is to try to cut down my carbon footprint in everyday life. For example, I go to school by bike or public transportation, like subway instead of driving a car. I always turn off lights when I leave the room; I try my best to use less plastic bags when shopping, as I always take a cloth bag with me when I go out.

Part 2

1. Describe an environment issue in your city.
   You should say:
   What it is;
   How it is caused;

What it results in;
And offer some solutions to the problem.

▶ **Sample Answer**

Although there are a multitude of environmental issues, I think global warming is one of the most concerning. So I'm going to talk about that.

First of all, as you probably know, global warming refers to the warming of earth's temperature. I've heard that temperatures could increase by over 10 degrees over the next century. It's certainly a worrying issue for scientists and the general population.

Honestly! I'm not an expert on this topic but as far as I know, carbon dioxide contributes greatly to this problem. Carbon dioxide and other pollutants are released by vehicles and factories on a daily basis. As a result, heat from the sun becomes trapped. If I remember correctly, this is called the greenhouse effect.

As a consequence of global warming, glaciers are melting, resulting in rising sea levels and flooding in some areas. Supposedly, it also considerably affects weather conditions too, making storms significantly more dangerous. I've even read that in some countries people have died due to rising temperatures.
It is a tough issue to tackle as we rely on cars and motorbikes to get from place to place. However, I guess a possible solution is technology. Now, various car manufacturers have begun designing and producing eco-friendly vehicles. Furthermore, using renewable energy instead of fossil fuels could help to reduce pollution levels considerably.

2. Describe a natural disaster that has occurred in your country.
   You should say:
   What is was;
   When it was;
   What destruction it caused;
   And explain how it made you feel.

3. Describe a type of public transportation in your city.
   You should say:
   What it is;

What the advantages are;

What the disadvantages are;

And offer some alternatives to this form of public transportation.

Part 3

1. What are the environmental effects of urbanization?

2. What are the main causes of pollution in your area?

3. How concerned are you about the environment?

4. How noticeable is the problem of deforestation in your country?

5. How has the environment changed since you were a child?

6. Are you optimistic about the future of our environment?

7. How can we strike a balance between development and protection?

8. Which is more important, increasing the standard of living or protecting the environment?

9. Tell me about some of the environmental problems that are affecting countries these days?

10. Do you think that governments around the world are doing enough to tackle the problems?

11. Why do some people not consider environmental problems to be serious?

12. What do you consider to be the world's worst environmental disaster caused by humans?

▶ Sample Answer

9. Tell me about some of the environmental problems that are affecting countries these days?

Well, there are a lot at the moment. Although it has not been proven for sure, there is a great deal of consensus about the fact that global warming is leading to severe weather change and this is resulting in many problems. We are seeing a lot of countries with the same problems that they have always had but on a much larger scale. For example, in the United States there seem to be far more hurricanes and tornadoes than in the past, with more devastating effects. There seems to constantly be news of serious flooding in many countries from Asia to Europe. Forest fires also seem to be getting worse, particularly each year in Australia and north America.

10. Do you think that governments around the world are doing enough to tackle the problems?

No, usually I don't think they are doing enough. There are countries that do what they can do help their people when problems occur and they are trying to come up with measures to mitigate the effects but when it comes to the major issue of global warming countries are not doing enough. It's hard to reach an agreement on how to reduce carbon footprints. Developed countries won't give up their habitual life style and government is not seriously concerned about this habitual life style that is very much environment-unfriendly. And the developing countries at the same time has this very need to provide a better life for their people. This actually is a difficult thing to balance for every country when tackling this problem across the whole world.

11. Why do some people not consider environmental problems to be serious?

I think there are several reasons for that. In some cases, it is simply because people are not affected on a day-to-day basis so it does not concern them. They just see it on the news affecting other people. It does not mean they do not care but they will soon forget about it. Also, some big organizations can be responsible for putting the wrong information out. For example, oil companies have a vested interest in making sure people do not believe in global warming as it could affect their profits, so they play the issue down. Also, some people think as it is a long-term problem, so they think it is not important for them since it will not affect them in near-future.

12. What do you consider to be the world's worst environmental disaster caused by humans?

I think that may be the nuclear disaster in Chernobyl, Ukraine. In that case there was an explosion and nuclear meltdown. It caused great loss of life. The environment was badly affected and it is still affected today and could be for many years. There are also many people who are still getting sick from the disaster and no one can live anywhere near the site. Of course there are many other serious ones, some more recent such as the nuclear leakage in Japan caused by earthquake and tsunami.

Checklist for This Chapter

Please check according to the scale from 1 to 5.

(1 — Strongly Disagree; 2 — Disagree; 3 — Undecided; 4 —Agree; 5 — Strongly Agree)

Can-do List	1	2	3	4	5
I know what IELTS Speaking Test Part 1 is.					
I know how to extend answers.					
I know how to clarify and confirm ideas.					
I know how to pronounce better.					
I understand the notion of eco-environment conservation in China.					

Self-reflection

1. In which part have I done very well?

2. In which part should I make improvement?

3. What should I do to bridge the current gap?

4. What suggestions do I have for my teacher or the class arrangement?

5. Anything I would like to say.

(Your reflection could be written in Chinese)

3

News and Media

LEARNING OBJECTIVES

In this chapter you will learn

- what IELTS Speaking Test Part 2 is like
- how to describe news and media
- how to express likes and dislikes
- how to use fillers strategy in IELTS Speaking Test
- the significance of holding a dialectic view towards information from the news and media

Part One   Warming-up

Task 1   *List four major influences social media has brought to your life in the chart below.*

1.

2.

3.

4.

07

Task 2 *Listen to a short presentation about the pros and cons of social media. Complete the sentences using words from the recording.*

1. Social media has positive mental health effects in terms of _____ and _____ people.

2. Social media have provided new platforms for _____ and _____ behaviors.

3. Social media platforms nurture and expand relationships, they _____, they _____ for mental health information and support.

4. _____ are particularly at risk because they are _____, and have different ideas about what should be kept _____ and what constitutes _____.

5. Other concerns of social media: Social media are _____; Social media invite us to _____; Social media harm _____; Social media allow _____ to spread quickly.

Task 3 Please list the differences between Newspaper and Weibo. You may discuss with your partners and compare your discussion results with other groups.

NO.	Newspaper	Weibo
1		
2		
3		
4		

Part Two   IELTS Speaking Test

General Introduction to IELTS Speaking Test Part 2

In IELTS Speaking Test Part 2, the examiner will give you a cue card or a task card which will consist of three or four questions along with some instructions on how to answer the topics. Once you get the topic, you'll be given one minute to prepare yourself on the given topic, after which you will have to speak for around 1 to 2 minutes until the examiner asks you to stop. Here, the examiner will check your usage of grammar and vocabulary, and your ability to frame sentences while talking. Speaking for 2 minutes may seem like a long time if you haven't practiced or if you're not used to speaking in English regularly. That is why it is advisable to practice well for the speaking test.

Tips for IELTS Speaking Test Part 2

■ **Read the card with the task carefully.**

Don't be in a hurry and don't skip this important step. If you misunderstand the task, your whole answer will not be correct. So, take your time and read the questions and bullet points attentively.

■ **Take advantage of one minute that you have for preparation.**

Some people advise to make notes on a sheet of paper during this minute. Others say that making notes is a waste of time, and it's better to make a plan of the answer in your head. You must choose the way that is the easiest for you. Try both techniques of preparation before the exam and find out which one you like more. If you decide to make notes, don't write full sentences as there is not enough time for this. You need to write only key words for the bullet points.

■ **Keep to the time limit.**

In this part, you will have to talk without stops for up to two minutes. When you prepare for the test, practice a lot in speaking for two minutes. Firstly, you will get the idea of how much you can say in two minutes. Secondly, you will get rid of the fear to talk for two minutes without stops. It's not advisable to stop speaking before the examiner tells you to do this. So, make sure you have enough ideas to talk about for this period of time.

IELTS Speaking Test Skills

■ **What are filler words?**

Filler words are words (and phrases) that are used to fill silence when you're speaking. They're words that don't add any real value to the sentence. They simply keep you going while you come up with the rest of your sentence. Their actual name is "discourse markers," but they are much more commonly known as "filler words." Since filler words don't really add any meaning to the sentence, you don't need to think about using them. This leaves your brain free to think of other things—like the word you're trying to remember.

■ When are filler words used in English?

You only need to use filler words when you're speaking out loud. Generally you won't use fillers when you're writing. When you're speaking out loud, though, you might need some extra time to figure out what to say. That's when you can use filler words. Filler words are used for a number of reasons.

1. *To show that you're thinking.*

   Use filler words when you need to think about your answer or statement. For example:

   "I have basi*cally...* ten more years of college."

2. *To make a statement less harsh.*

   When your friend has some broccoli stuck between his teeth, you could just tell him, "You have something in your teeth," but that might make him embarrassed. It might be nicer to say something more like: "Well, you have, um, you have a little something in your teeth."

3. *To make your statement weaker or stronger.*

   While filler words don't add anything to sentences, they can be used to change the sentence tone — the attitude of the sentence. See how different these three statements sound: "I think pugs are cute" is just a regular statement. "Actually, I think pugs are cute" shows contrast — that someone else doesn't agree. "At the end of the day, I think pugs are cute" is something you might say as a conclusion to a discussion about pugs and their ugly (or cute!) wrinkles.

4. *To stall for time.*

   To stall for time means to do something to try and gain more time. Filler words are an excellent way to stall when you don't know how to answer a question, or when you don't want to. For example, if your teacher asks you "Where's your homework?", your response might sound a bit like this: "*Uhh. Umm. Well, you see.* My dog ate it."

5. *To include the listener in the conversation without ending your sentence.*

   A conversation takes at least two people. Some filler words and phrases can include the other person in the conversation. It's a bit like reaching out to them as you're speaking to keep their attention. For example: "It was a really big bear, *you know*?"

Task 1   *Please read the following table and tell the function of each filler words.*

Fillers Words & Examples	Functions
"Well" ■ *Well*, I guess $20 is a good price for a pair of jeans. ■ The apples and cinnamon go together like, *well*, apples and cinnamon. ■ *Well* .... fine, you can borrow my car.	
"Um" or "uh" ■ *Um*, I *uh* thought the project was due tomorrow, not today. ■ *Umm* ... I like the yellow dress better!	
"Like" ■ My neighbor has *like* ten dogs. ■ My friends was *like*, completely ready to *like* kick me out of the car if I didn't stop laughing.	
"Actually / Basically / Seriously" ■ *Actually*, pugs are really cute! ■ "*Basically*, the last Batman movie was *seriously* exciting!" ■ "*Clearly* you *totally* didn't see me, even though I was *literally* in front of your face."	
"You see" or "You know" ■ "I was going to try the app, but *you see*, I ran out of space on my phone." ■ "We stayed at that hotel, *you know*, the one down the street from Times Square."	
"I mean" ■ "*I mean*, he's a great guy, I'm just not sure if he's a good doctor." ■ "The duck and the tiger were awesome but scary. *I mean*, the tiger was scary, not the duck."	
"You know what I mean" ■ "I really like that girl, *you know what I mean*?"	

Fillers Words & Examples	Functions
"At the end of the day" ■ "*At the end of the day*, we're all just humans, and we all make mistakes."	
"Believe me" ■ "*Believe me*, this is the cheapest, tiniest house ever!"	
"I guess"/ "I suppose" ■ "I was going to eat dinner at home, but *I guess* I can go eat at a restaurant instead."	
"Right/mhm/uh huh" ■ *Right*, so let's prepare a list of all the things we'll need." ■ "*Uh huh*, that's exactly what he told me too."	

https://www.fluentu.com/english/

Task 2　*Please make up short conversations about the following topics with your partners. Use proper filler words in your conversations.*

1. my favorite TV program
2. the most popular news coverage
3. the influence of WeChat for the old generation
4. the APP you recommend to get news

Part Three　Speaking after Reading

Children and Advertising

Young children are trusting of commercial advertisements in the media, and advertisers have sometimes been accused of taking advantage of this trusting outlook. The Independent Television Commission, regulator of television advertising in the United Kingdom, has criticized advertisers for "misleadingness" — creating a wrong impression either intentionally or unintentionally — in an effort to control advertisers' use of techniques that make it difficult for children to judge the true size, action, performance, or construction of a toy.

General concern about misleading tactics that advertisers employ is centered on the use of exaggeration. Consumer protection groups and parents believe that children are largely ill-equipped to recognize such techniques and that often exaggeration is used at the expense of product information. Claims such as "the best" or "better than" can be subjective and misleading; even adults may be unsure as to their meaning. They represent the advertiser's opinions about the qualities of their products or brand and, as a consequence, are difficult to verify. Advertisers sometimes offset or counterbalance an exaggerated claim with a disclaimer — a qualification or condition on the claim. For example, the claim that breakfast cereal has a health benefit may be accompanied by the disclaimer "when part of a nutritionally balanced breakfast." However, research has shown that children often have difficulty understanding disclaimers: children may interpret the phrase "when part of a nutritionally balanced breakfast" to mean that the cereal is required as a necessary part of a balanced breakfast. The author George Comstock suggested that less than a quarter of children between the ages of six and eight years old understood standard disclaimers used in many toy advertisements and that disclaimers are more readily comprehended when presented in both audio and visual formats. Nevertheless, disclaimers are mainly presented in audio format only.

Fantasy is one of the more common techniques in advertising that could possibly mislead a young audience. Child-oriented advertisements are more likely to include magic and fantasy than advertisements aimed at adults. In a content analysis of Canadian television, the author Stephen Kline observed that nearly all commercials for character toys featured fantasy play. Children have strong imaginations and the use of fantasy brings their ideas to life, but children may not be adept enough to realize that what they are viewing is unreal. Fantasy situations and settings are frequently used to attract children's attention, particularly in food advertising. Advertisements for breakfast cereals have, for many years, been found to be especially fond of fantasy techniques, with almost nine out of ten including such content. Generally, there is uncertainty as to whether very young children can distinguish between fantasy and reality in advertising. Certainly, rational appeals in advertising aimed at children are limited, as most advertisements use emotional and indirect appeals to psychological states or associations.

The use of celebrities such as singers and movie stars is common in advertising. The intention is for the positively perceived attributes of the celebrity to be transferred to the advertised product and for the two to become automatically linked in the audience's mind. In children's advertising, the "celebrities" are often animated figures from popular cartoons. In the recent past, the role of celebrities in advertising to children has often been conflated with the concept of host selling. Host selling involves blending advertisements with regular programming in a way that makes it difficult to distinguish one from the other. Host selling occurs, for example, when a children's show about a cartoon lion contains an ad in which the same lion promotes a breakfast cereal. The psychologist Dale Kunkel showed that the practice of host selling reduced children's ability to distinguish between advertising and program material. It was also found that older children responded more positively to products in host selling advertisements.

Regarding the appearance of celebrities in advertisements that do not involve host selling, the evidence is mixed. Researcher Charles Atkin found that children believe that the characters used to advertise breakfast cereals are knowledgeable about cereals, and children accept such characters as credible sources of nutritional information. This finding was even more marked for heavy viewers of television. In addition, children feel validated in their choice of a product when a celebrity endorses that product. A study of children in Hong Kong, however, found that the presence of celebrities in advertisements could negatively affect the children's perceptions of a product if the children did not like the celebrity in question.

Word Bank

regulator	*n.* a person or body that supervises a particular industry or business activity 管理者；管理机构
tactics	*n.* the science and art of disposing and maneuvering forces in combat 战术；策略
exaggeration	*n.* a statement or description that makes sth larger, better, or worse or more important than it really is 夸张
counterbalance	*n.* an equivalent counterbalancing weight 抗衡
disclaimer	*n.* (law) a voluntary repudiation of a person's legal claim to something; denial of any connection with or knowledge of 否认声明；放弃；免责声明
nutritionally	*adv.* with regard to nutrition 在营养上
rational	*adj.* based on reason rather than emotions 理性的
animated	*adj.* having life or vigor or spirit 活泼的，生机勃勃的
conflate	*vt.* mix together different elements 合并，混合

Task 1 *Read the article and pick up the best choice.*

1. Which of the following is NOT mentioned in paragraph 1 as being a difficult judgment for children to make about advertised toys?

   A) how big the toys are

   B) how much the toys cost

   C) what the toys can do

   D) how the toys are made

2. What is suggested in the statement of cereal advertisements about "when part of a nutritionally balanced breakfast"?

   A) The cereal is a desirable part of a healthful, balanced breakfast.

   B) The cereal contains equal amounts of all nutrients.

   C) Cereal is a healthier breakfast than other foods are.

   D) The cereal is the most nutritious part of the breakfast meal.

3. According to paragraph 2, which statement is untrue of disclaimers made in advertisements?

   A) They are qualifications or conditions put on a claim.

   B) They may be used to balance exaggerations.

   C) They are usually presented in both audio and visual formats.

   D) They are often difficult for children to understand.

4. Paragraph 3 indicates that there is uncertainty about which of the following issues involving children and fantasy in advertising?

   A) whether children can tell if what they are seeing in an advertisement is real or fantasy

   B) whether children can differentiate fantasy techniques from other techniques used in advertising

   C) whether children realize how commonly fantasy techniques are used in advertising aimed at them

   D) whether children are attracted to advertisements that lack fantasy

5. In paragraph 4, why does the author mention a show about a cartoon lion in which an advertisement appears featuring the same lion character?

   A) to help explain what is meant by the term "host selling" and why it can be misleading to children

   B) to explain why the role of celebrities in advertising aimed at children has often been confused with host selling

   C) to compare the effectiveness of using animated figures with the effectiveness of using celebrities in advertisements aimed at children

   D) to indicate how Kunkel first became interested in studying the effects of host selling on children

Task 2 *Please share ideas with your partners about the following questions based on what you read.*

1. Can you list at least 3 facts to show the influence of advertising on children?

2. Can you give one example to show the necessity of banning advertising from young children under the age of 12?

3. Why are children influenced more by advertisement than adults?

Task 3 *Suppose you are a candidate for an advertising company. You are required to plan a piece of advertise of a newly-produced pen. Please report to your partners about your plan with the help of a poster you designed. You may consider the following points:*

- What's new in the pen?
- Who are the target consumers?
- How to advertise the product (advertisement putting; slogan; spokesperson)?

Part Four   Speaking after Listening

IELTS Speaking Skill — Expressing Likes and Dislikes

- **Talking about likes**

  I like classical music a lot/very much.

  I came to like swimming.

  I've started to like Chinese food.

  I've come to like baseball.

  I love reading in my spare time.

  I enjoy walking alone in the park after dinner.

  I'm fond of reality shoe.

  I'm enthusiastic about play basketball.

  I can't find words to express how much I like it.

You can also use the following drills

  I'm keen on ...

  I'm crazy about ...

  I'm pleased with ...

  I'm satisfied with ...

  I'm interested in ...

I'm content with ...

I'm hooked on ...

I'm addicted to ...

I've developed a great liking for ...

I'm really a fan of ...

... grows on me.

... appeals to me.

... is my favorite.

■ Talking about dislikes

I don't like eating alone.

I don't particularly like speaking in public.

I don't like the idea of travelling so long.

I hate my boss!

I dislike being yelled at.

You don't seem like watching TV series.

You can also use the following drills

I don't care for ...

I don't feel like ...

I'm not fond of ...

I have a dislike of ...

I can't stand ...

I can hardly bear ...

I can't put up with ...

I can't say I like ...

I've got tired of ...

... is boring.

... is just so-so.

They make my stomach turn.

They're not for me.

I can't take it.

It's driving me crazy.

■ Asking about likes and dislikes

Do you like roses?

Do you like this writer in particular?

Do you enjoy reading?

Are you keen on stamp collection?

Do you care for rock-and-roll?

You can also use the following drills

How about ...?

What about ...?

How do you like ...?

What do you think about / of ...?

What... do you like best?

What is your favorite ...?

Task 1　*The following items contain important vocabulary from the lecture. Work with a partner and match vocabulary terms with their definitions. Check your answers in a dictionary if necessary.*

1. The incident has received wide **coverage** in the press.

2. University funding was **tremendously** biased toward scientists.

3. Don't believe all the **gossip** you hear.

4. These results are a further **proof** of his outstanding ability.

5. NATO defense ministers **wrap up** their meeting in Brussels today.

a. information, documents, etc. that show that sth is true

b. informal talk or stories about other people's private lives, that may be unkind or not true

c. the reporting of news and sport in newspapers and on the radio and television

d. complete it in a satisfactory way

e. to emphasize how strong a feeling or quality is, or how large an amount is

Task 2　*Listen to the lecture and pick up the best choice.*

1. What do scientists tell us about humans and famous people?

　A) Scientists tell us that human beings are naturally interested in famous people.

　B) Scientists find out that all human beings want to become famous.

　C) Scientists believe famous people have to attract human beings very hard.

　D) Scientists think it is difficult to make human beings to be interested in famous people.

2. Why has news coverage gone down by about 10% in the last 25 years?

    A) This is because people are no longer interested in news.

    B) This is because there are too many fake news reports.

    C) This is because the media has more coverage of celebrity news.

    D) This is because more and more people think it is meaningless to read such information.

3. Which one is the reason for the increase in the amount of celebrity coverage?

    A) Newspapers with celebrity coverage can sell with higher price.

    B) Newspapers discovered that celebrity news helps them sell more papers.

    C) Newspaper editors admire celebrities.

    D) Celebrities would like to pay for being on the coverage of newspaper.

4. What is the negative result of the increase in celebrity coverage?

    A) Children know much less about world and local events.

    B) Children cannot distinguish real world from virtual world.

    C) Children talk too much about celebrities with their friends.

    D) Children may dream about becoming celebrities.

Task 3   *Please discuss with your partners about the following questions. Try to use expressions of expressing likes and dislikes discussed in the previous part. You can do peer or self-evaluation by using the criteria below.*

1. How big a problem is the increase in celebrity coverage?

2. What are some possible positive effects in celebrity coverage?

3. What is the best way to learn about celebrity?

4. Tell each other a time when you or your friend saw a celebrity. What happened? How did you feel?

Criteria for Peer- / Self-Assessment

NO.	Analytic Items	Proportion	Peer- /Self-Assessment
1	Using proper expressions of expressing likes and dislikes	20%	
2	Fluency (less accidental pauses, short pause length, less self-correction)	20%	
3	Accuracy (accuracy in using words and expressions, accuracy in grammar use)	20%	

NO.	Analytic Items	Proportion	Peer- /Self-Assessment
4	Complexity(lexical variety, usage of less frequent vocabulary, syntactic complexity)	20%	
5	Pronunciation (no strong accent, correct stress, liaison, plosion in words and sentences, sounds naturally)	20%	
Total Score (use a 10-point scale)			

Part Five   Critical Thinking

Making the Headlines

It isn't very often that the media lead with the same story everywhere in the world. Such an event would have to be of enormous international significance. But this is exactly what occurred in September 2001 with the terrorist attack on the Twin Towers of the World Trade Center in New York. It is probably not exaggerated to say that from that moment the world was a different place.

But it is not just the historical and international dimension that made 9/11 memorable and (to use a word the media like) newsworthy. It was the shock and horror too. So striking, so sensational, was the news that, years after the event , many people can still remember exactly where they were and what they were doing when they first heard it. They can remember their own reactions: For many people across the globe their first instinct was to go and tell someone else about it, thus providing confirmation of the old saying that bad news travels fast.

And so it is with all major news stories. I remember when I was at primary school the teacher announcing pale-faced to a startled class of seven-year-olds President Kennedy is dead. I didn't know who President Kennedy was, but I was so upset at hearing the news that I went rushing home afterwards to tell my parents (who already knew, of course). In fact, this is one of my earliest memories.

So what exactly is news? The objective importance of an event is obviously not enough — there are plenty of enormous global issues out there, with dramatic consequences, from poverty to global warming — but since they are ongoing, they don't all make the headlines on the same day. 9/11, in contrast, was not just international, but odd, unexpected, and (in the sense that it was possible to identify with the plight of people caught up in the drama) very human.

Odd doesn't mean huge. Take the story in the *China Daily* about a mouse holding up a flight from Vietnam to Japan. The mouse was spotted running down the aisle of a plane in Hanoi airport. It was eventually caught by a group of 12 technicians worried that the mouse could chew through wires and cause a short circuit. By the time it took off the plane was more than four hours late.

Not an event with momentous international consequences, you might say, (apart from a few passengers arriving late for their appointments in another country), but there are echoes of the story across the globe, in online editions of papers from Asia to America, and even Scotland ("Mouse Chase Holds up Flight", in the *Edinburgh Evening News*).

Another element of newsworthiness is immediacy. This refers to the nearness of the event in time. An event which happened a week ago is not generally news — unless you've just read about it. "When" is one of the five "wh" questions trainee journalists are regularly told that they have to use to frame a news story (the others are "who", "what", "where" and "why"); "today", "this morning", and "yesterday" are probably at the top of the list of time adverbs in a news report. Similarly, an event which is about to happen ("today", "this evening" or "tonight") may also be newsworthy, although, by definition, it is not unexpected and so less sensational.

When it comes to immediacy, those media which can present news in real time, such as TV, radio, and the Internet, have an enormous advantage over the press. To see an event unfolding in front of your eyes is rather different from reading about it at breakfast the next morning. But TV news is not necessarily more objective or reliable than a newspaper report, since the images you are looking at on your screen have been chosen by journalists or editors with specific objectives, or at least following set guidelines, and they are shown from a unique viewpoint. By placing the camera somewhere else you would get a different picture. This is why it is usual to talk of the "power of the media" — the power to influence the public, more or less covertly.

But perhaps in the third millennium this power is being eroded, or at least devolved to ordinary people. The proliferation of personal blogs, the possibility of self-broadcasting through sites such as YouTube, and the growth of open-access web pages (wikis) means that anyone with anything to say — or show — can now reach a worldwide audience instantly.

This doesn't mean that the press and TV are going to disappear overnight, of course. But in their never-ending search for interesting news items — odd, unexpected, and human — they are going to turn increasingly to these sites for their sources, providing the global information network with a curiously local dimension.

Task 1   *Work in pairs and discuss the questions.*

1. What do you think make a story newsworthy?
2. What are the problems facing journalists who want to be objective?
3. In what way are the media powerful?
4. Do you think the media are too powerful?
5. If anyone can publish news on the Internet, is this a good thing?

Task 2   *Read the quotes about the news and decide which ones you agree with. Share your ideas with your partners.*

1. When a dog bites a man, it usually doesn't make news. But if a man bites a dog, that is news. (John B. Bogart)
2. News is what a chap who doesn't care much about anything wants to read. And it's only news until he's read it. After that, it's dead. (Evelyn Waugh)
3. News is what somebody somewhere wants to suppress; all the rest is advertising. (Lord Northcliffe)
4. Nothing travels faster than light, with the possible exception of bad news. (Dauglas Adams)
5. No news is good news. (Proverb)

Task 3   *The picture below is the study result of media use among young people. Discuss with your partner how does your use of media compare to that of 8- to 18-year olds in the study.*

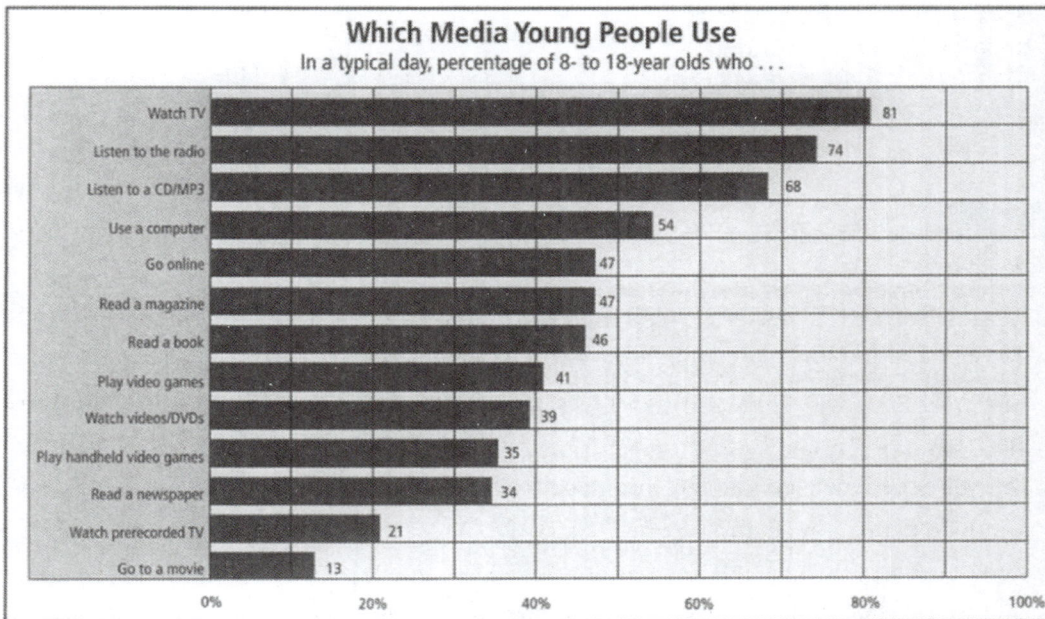

Which Media Young People Use
In a typical day, percentage of 8- to 18-year olds who . . .

Media	Percentage
Watch TV	81
Listen to the radio	74
Listen to a CD/MP3	68
Use a computer	54
Go online	47
Read a magazine	47
Read a book	46
Play video games	41
Watch videos/DVDs	39
Play handheld video games	35
Read a newspaper	34
Watch prerecorded TV	21
Go to a movie	13

0%   20%   40%   60%   80%   100%

Task 4   *Listen to a lecture about learning and fill the following sentences according to what you hear.*

1. So, today we're going to focus just on Internet news. And my focus today is on ... is on the research _____.
2. One thing they found was that _____.
3. Well, first of all, I want you to notice is the ... the increase in the number of people _____, you know, things like wars, deaths of important people, and so forth.
4. So, the bottom line is that _____.

Task 5   *In group of four, read the following questions and discuss them with your group members.*

1. What kind of information can you get from the Internet?
   Possible ideas:

   news   shopping   stock quotes   sports   health   information
   weather   advice   local activities

2. Why is it important to get the news?

Possible ideas:

to help make decisions

to be prepared for the change

to know about the world

to have something to talk about with friends

Task 6   *Please share your idea with your partners about one of the following statements.*

1. The lecture points out that Internet news is current, complete, and interactive. When have you found this may not be true? Give examples.

2. Can you give one more positive or negative aspect of Internet news that you have noticed?

3. In your experience, do you feel young people know enough about current world events? Can you explain in detail?

4. Look back at your notes. What was another idea in the lecture that you found important and interesting? Tell the class why you think it is important or interesting and ask for their opinions.

Part Six   Encountering IELTS Speaking

Words and Expressions about Media

accredited journalist 特派记者

advertisement 广告

advance 预发消息；预写消息

affair 桃色新闻；绯闻

anecdote 趣闻轶事

assignment 采写任务

attribution 消息出处，消息来源

back alley news 小道消息

back grounding 新闻背景

Bad news travels quickly. 坏事传千里。

banner 通栏标题

beat 采写范围

blank "开天窗"

body 新闻正文

boil 压缩（篇幅）

box 花边新闻

brief 简讯

bulletin 新闻简报

byline 署名文章

caption 图片说明

caricature 漫画

carry 刊登

cartoon 漫画

censor 审查（新闻稿件），新闻审查

chart 每周流行音乐排行榜

clipping 剪报

column 专栏；栏目

columnist 专栏作家

continued story 连载故事；连载小说

contributing editor 特约编辑

contribution （投给报刊的）稿件；投稿

contributor 投稿人

copy desk 新闻编辑部

copy editor 文字编辑

correction 更正（启事）

correspondence column 读者来信专栏

correspondent 驻外记者；常驻外埠记者

cover 采访；采写

cover girl 封面女郎

covert coverage 隐性采访；秘密采访

crop 剪辑（图片）

crusade 宣传攻势

cut 插图；删减（字数）

cut line 插图说明

layout 版面编排；版面设计

lead 导语

libel 诽谤（罪）

makeup 版面设计

man of the year 年度新闻人物，年度风云人物

mass communication 大众传播（学）

mass media 大众传播媒介

master head 报头；报名

media 媒介，媒体

Mere report is not enough to go upon. 仅是传闻不足为凭。

morgue 报刊资料室

news agency 通讯社

news clue 新闻线索

news peg 新闻线索，新闻电头

newsprint 新闻纸

news value 新闻价值

No news is good news. 没有消息就是好消息。（不闻凶讯便是吉。）

daily 日报

dateline 新闻电头

deadline 截稿时间

dig 深入采访；追踪（新闻线索）；"挖"（新闻）

digest 文摘

editorial 社论

editorial office 编辑部

editors notes 编者按

exclusive 独家新闻

expose 揭丑新闻；新闻曝光

extra 号外

eye-account 目击记；记者见闻

faxed photo 传真照片

feature 特写；专稿

feedback 信息反馈

file 发送消息；发稿

filler 补白

First Amendment （美国宪法）第一修正案（内容有关新闻、出版自由等）

five "Wh" of news 新闻五要素

flag 报头；报名

folo (=follow-up) 连续报道

Fourth Estate 第四等级（新闻界的别称）

freedom of the Press 新闻自由

free-lancer 自由撰稿人

full position 醒目位置

Good news comes on crutches. 好事不出

门。

grapevine 小道消息

gutter 中缝

hard news 硬新闻；纯消息

headline 新闻标题；内容提要

hearsay 小道消息

highlights 要闻

hot news 热点新闻

human interest 人情味

in-depth reporting 深度报道

insert 插补段落；插稿

interpretative reporting 解释性报道

invasion of privacy 侵犯隐私（权）

inverted pyramid 倒金字塔（写作结构）

investigative reporting 调查性报道

journalism 新闻业；新闻学

journalist 新闻记者

kill 退弃（稿件）；枪毙（稿件）

obituary 讣告

objectivity 客观性

off the record 不宜公开报道

opinion poll 民意测验

periodical 期刊

pipeline 匿名消息来源

popular paper 大众化报纸；通俗报纸

press 报界；新闻界

press conference 新闻发布会；记者招待会

press law 新闻法

press release 新闻公告；新闻简报

PR man 公关先生

profile 人物专访；人物特写

proofreader 校对员

pseudo event 假新闻

nose for news 新闻敏感

IELTS Speaking Skill — Fluency and Coherence

The IELTS speaking assessment criteria covers four main areas of speaking. The first of these is fluency and coherence (see Table 3–1). According to the descriptor, "fluency and coherence assesses how well you can speak at a normal speed without too much hesitation." That means how well you are able to discuss the topic **without** pausing or hesitating too much or repeating the same words.

To get a high score for this section you have to develop your answers and organize your ideas logically. Now what do I mean by organizing ideas? Well take a look at this example:

[Examiner] *Do you think we are healthier now than what we used to be 100 years ago*?

[The student] *We are healthier in some ways and we are less healthy in some other ways*.

This is a poor answer to this question.

Now let's check another answer with a higher score:

［The student］ *Well, I believe that generally, we are more health-conscious, but I think in some ways we are less healthy than in the past.*

Did you notice in the second answer how the speaker organized her idea with using connecting phrases like:

Well, I believe ...

Generally, ...

But I think ...

Table 3–1 Band Descriptor of Frequency in IELTS Speaking Test

Score	Frequency
9	• speaks fluently with only rare repetition or self-correction • any hesitation is content-related rather than to find words or grammar • speaks coherently with fully appropriate cohesive features • develops topics fully and appropriately
8	• speaks fluently with only occasional repetition or self-correction; hesitation is usually content-related and only rarely to search for language • develops topics coherently and appropriately
7	• speaks at length without noticeable effort or loss of coherence • may demonstrate language-related hesitation at times, or some repetition and/or self-correction • uses a range of connectives and discourse markers with some flexibility
6	• is willing to speak at length, though may lose coherence at times due to occasional repetition, self-correction or hesitation • uses a range of connectives and discourse markers but not always appropriately
5	• usually maintains flow of speech but uses repetition, self-correction and/or slow speech to keep going • may over-use certain connectives and discourse markers • produces simple speech fluently, but more complex communication causes fluency problems

https://www.ielts.org/-/media/pdfs/speaking-band-descriptors.ashx?la=en

Task 1 *Please tell your partner what you usually get from the Internet by considering fluency and coherence. You can jot down notes in the following box.*

Task 2 *Please tell your partner which kind of media you prefer the most and why by considering fluency and coherence in speaking.*

The Media I prefer	Reasons

IELTS Speaking Test Items

Part 1

1. Do many people have cable TV in your country?

2. Are there many cinemas in your city?

3. Do you prefer to watch a movie at home or at the movie theatre?

4. Which are you more interested in, local or international news?

5. Why are people interested in news?

6. Should you always keep up with the latest news?

7. Where do you get your news from?

8. What's the difference between news from the radio and that from TV?

9. When and where do you read newspaper?

▶ **Sample Answer**

3. Do you prefer to watch a movie at home or at the movie theatre?

I definitely like going to the movie theatre more. I really love the whole experience of buying some drinks and popcorns and going with friends and watching it on the big screen. I just saw a 3D movie, a horror movie and it was fantastic.

Part 2

1. Describe a newspaper you enjoy reading.

You should say:

What the newspaper is;

What sections it has;

When and how often you read it;

And express why you like it.

▶ **Sample Answer**

I would like to introduce my favorite newspaper today. It's called *The Youth*. I didn't start reading it until I was in high school. I would read the paper on weekends. The paper has every section that normal newspapers have. It has news about national and international events. In addition, it has a wonderful travel section that has articles from all over the world and it offers perspectives that you don't get in normal newspaper. It also has a very interesting section: word game section. Many interesting word games can be found in this section, such as "Words within Words" where the aim is to make as many words as possible with the letters of a single word. On Sundays, it has a special supplement. It has a magazine that comes with it and my favorite article is in there. It's all about language and it puts together the history of words and it explains why we say the things we do. I only read it once a week now because I don't have much time with work and all. But when I do read it, I like to sit down at my computer and have a nice cup of tea and I take a couple of hours to read it actually. I really enjoy catching up on all the news because I think it's interesting to know more about the world. I also like seeing all the news about the travel and possible places I might take vacations in the future because usually they're places I wouldn't even think about, like going to beautiful

2. Describe a TV or radio ad you like.

You should say:

What the product is;

How it is promoted;

What makes it different from other ads;

And explain why you like it.

3. Describe a recent news event.

You should say:

What it was;

When it happened;

Where it happened;

And explain how you felt when you heard about it.

Part 3

1. Outline what role newspaper play in our society these days.

2. Evaluate how much influence that media has over young people.

3. Comment on how much the media has contributed to globalization.

4. To what extent should we trust the media?

5. What news must people know about? What do they not need to know?

6. How has the media developed over the past 50 years?

7. How are newspapers different these days compared to the past?

8. Should the media be censored?

9. Is there too much advertising on the TV?

10. Do you think tabloids should be banned?

▶ **Sample Answer**

1. Outline what role newspaper play in our society these days.

Well, I think newspapers are still important despite what many people say.

I think they offer different news on politics and a lot of people still depend on newspapers to get their ideas about what laws should be passed and who they should vote for. They also play an important social role. They list all the activities that you can do over the weekend with your family or friends and what concerts and other art events are coming to town.

2. Evaluate how much influence that media has over young people.

Oh, they have a lot of influence, a great deal of influence on young people. Young people love to listen to the latest music, to the pop music that everyone else likes or to follow the fashion trends. Therefore they have to look at the magazines to see what their favourite singer is wearing or what the movie stars wore at the academy awards for example, and they want to look like that. They want to look like famous people so they dress like the people they see in the media. Also if they see a celebrity is maybe interested in a new type of music or a new issue then they'll try to learn more about that. So the media, yeah, they have a lot of influence over young people.

3. Comment on how much the media has contributed to globalization.

Well that's a difficult question. Let me give you an example. Coca-Cola is a good example. Coca-Cola is everywhere. Products like that, that you can find in any small village in Mexico or any big city in China, it's the same product, it's the same company and that's part of globalization and the reason why people know about these products is due to the media, is due to advertising. Like I mentioned before, people follow celebrities. When celebrities endorse products, it makes people want to buy them. So advertising, I think just advertising in the media has contributed to globalization.

Checklist for This Chapter

Please check according to the scale from 1 to 5.

(1 — Strongly Disagree; 2 — Disagree; 3 — Undecided; 4 —Agree; 5 — Strongly Agree)

Can-do List	1	2	3	4	5
I know what IELTS Speaking Test Part 2 is.					
I can use filler words properly in speaking.					
I know how to express likes and dislikes.					
I can speak fluently and coherently.					
I know the significance of holding a dialectic view towards information from the news and media.					

Self-reflection

1. In which part have I done very well?

2. In which part should I make improvement?

3. What should I do to bridge the current gap?

4. What suggestions do I have for my teacher or the class arrangement?

5. Anything I would like to say.

(Your reflection could be written in Chinese)

Celebrity

LEARNING OBJECTIVES

In this chapter you will learn

- how to describe people
- how to summarize people's deeds chronologically
- how to express agreement and disagreement
- the value of selfless dedication and the qualities leading to success

Part One   Warming-up

Task 1   *List three famous people whom you admire. Tell your partner why you admire one of them. You may jot down the key words in the following box while preparing for your speaking.*

> 1.
>
> 2.
>
> 3.

Task 2 *Listen to a short presentation about "Albert Einstein", then fill the blanks in the following sentences.*

1. Albert Einstein was a _____, although most people probably know him as _____ who ever lived.

2. He must have been _____ the Theory of Relativity and the equation E=mc^2.

3. In 1999, *Time* magazine named Einstein as _____. No one could have guessed this would happen when he was at school. He was extremely interested in science but hated the system of learning by heart. He said _____. He had already done many experiments, but failed the entrance exams to a technical college.

4. He didn't let this setback stop him. When he was 16, he performed his famous experiment of _____. He eventually graduated from university, in 1900, with a degree in physics. Twelve years later he was a university professor and in 1921, he won the Nobel Prize for Physics. He went on to publish over 300 scientific papers.

5. Einstein is the only scientist to _____, a household name, and _____. He once joked that when people stopped him in the street, he always replied: "Pardon me, sorry! Always I am mistaken for Professor Einstein." Today, he is seen as _____, who just happened to change our world.

Task 3 *Please list the synonyms or the expressions having the same meaning to the following words and phrases.*

Words and Phrases	Synonyms/Expressions Having the Same Meaning
be pretty brainy to ...	
setback	
a cult figure	
a household name	
typical	

Talking about People

Many IELTS Part 2 Questions are relevant to describing people, such as celebrities, friends, family members, historical figures or even interesting strangers.

For example:

- describe one of your best friends
- describe a famous person you would like to meet
- describe a successful sports person that you like
- describe someone who offered you help before

There may be a lot of information to share about you and the one you described. You can refer to the following sentences, especially the expressions in boldface in your own description.

Here are some example phrases with different *prepositions*.

- We first met **at** a party/ **at** university.
- We met each other **through** a mutual friend/ family/work/video game.
- We were introduced **by** a friend of mine/ a colleague/ a teacher.

Here are some useful *(phrasal) verbs* to describe relationship.

- At first, we didn't really **get along**, but eventually we became good friends.
- In the beginning, we weren't close friends, but after we **got to know each other**, ...
- We weren't very close until we realized that we both **had a lot in common**.

***Superlative adjectives* are often used in this part.**

- Out of everyone in my family, my father has definitely **inspired me the most**.
- My mum is definitely one of **the most patient** people in my family.
- Out of all the historical figures in England, Lord Nelson **interests me the most**.

After you use a superlative adjective to describe someone, try to give a physical example that demonstrates that quality. Some flexible yet impressive phrases to use are *if, when* or *whenever*.

- He's very patient. **If** I am running late he never gets angry and always waits for me.
- She's one of the most creative people in my group of friends. **When** I was setting up my business, she helped me design a fantastic-looking logo which I still use today.
- Brian is just the funniest guy I know. Even **when** I'm feeling down, he can still cheer me up, or **if** we're in a bad situation, he can find the humor in it.

Generally, there are several steps to give your response in this part.

Example 1

Describe a famous person that you are interested in.

You should say:

Step 1. Who this person is

Step 2. How you got to know this person

Step 3. What sort of life he/she had before he/she became famous

Step 4. How this person became famous

Step 5. Why you like this person

Example 2

Describe a creative person that you admire.

You should say:

Step 1. Who this person is

Step 2. How you got to know this person

Step 3. What creative things this person likes to do

Step 4. Why you admire this person.

Task 1   *Describe one of the three famous people you've listed in Task 1 of Part One according to the steps mentioned above. Note down the key words and information while preparing for your description.*

Step 1. _____

_____

Step 2. _____

_____

Step 3. _____

_____

Step 4. _____

_____

Step 5. _____

_____

Task 2 *Work with your partners. Please take turns to describe a creative person that you admire. Note down the key words and information while preparing for your description.*

Step 1. _____

_____

Step 2. _____

_____

Step 3. _____

_____

Step 4. _____

_____

Part Three   Speaking after Reading

The Most Fragrant Rose — Zhang Guimei

Located in Huaping County in Lijiang, Southwest China's Yunnan Province, the Huaping High School for Girls is well-known not only because it is the first girls' public high school in the nation that does not charge tuition fees, but also for its high percentage of graduates who enter universities — last year, the school's university admission rate ranked first among all high schools in Lijiang.

None of this would have happened without Zhang Guimei. The 63-year-old has been fighting the inequality and prejudice girls face in the mountains for a long time.

In 2001, Zhang, then a teacher of local middle school, was appointed the part-time president of a center for homeless children in the county. She found many of the girls who lived at the center were abandoned by their parents. She also noticed many girls in the region, especially from poor families, had little chance of getting education.

In a conversation with one of her students' mother, Zhang learned the woman sent her son in junior middle school to an extracurricular training institution, but not her daughter who was soon going to take college entrance examination, because she thought it was more important for boys to study. These experiences inspired Zhang to establish a school for girls living in the mountainous areas, mainly those who are unable to continue their studies after completing the nine-year compulsory education. She was determined to make sure the school did not charge tuition fees.

To raise money for the school, between 2002 and 2007, Zhang spent the summer and winter vacations on the streets, asking people to donate for her school. Many people refused to donate and humiliated her, and Zhang only managed to collect about 10,000 yuan, which was nowhere near enough to start a school.

The turning point came in 2007. That year, Zhang was selected as a representative of the 17th CPC National Congress, and the local government issued a special grant for her to purchase some new clothes before she went to attend the meetings in Beijing. Instead, she used the money to buy computers for her students.

At the meeting, a reporter noticed Zhang was wearing jeans with holes in them, and reported her story. Since then, Zhang and her dream to start a school for girls have drawn attention from the public.

Consequently, governments of Lijiang city and Huaping County allocated one million yuan, respectively, to construct a school, and the Huaping High School for Girls was officially opened in September 2008. Funds for school operations and salaries of teaching staff are also covered by the local government. Zhang set a high academic standard for the school from the beginning. She asked teachers to ensure all graduates be admitted into colleges, regardless of their initial academic performances.

Difficulties soon followed. Many teachers considered Zhang's goal a mission impossible — the school did not set a minimum admission score when it enrolled the first batch of 100 students, and many students had a poor academic performance. Coupled with the school's humble conditions, six months after it opened, nine out of its 17 teachers offered to resign, which nearly paralyzed all school operations.

Disheartened by the reality, Zhang also prepared for the handover. As she was organizing the documents, she found six out of the eight remaining staff workers at the school were members of the Communist Party of China. Zhang gathered them and they reviewed the oath of joining the Party together in front of a Party flag they drew. Everyone burst into tears before they could finish the oath. The school did not shut down. Zhang and her colleagues spared no time and efforts to improve teaching at the school.

"I want my students to go to good universities. I want children in the mountainous regions to enter prestigious colleges such as Tsinghua University and Peking University," Zhang said. During the 12 years since the school was founded, over 1,600 girl students have graduated and received higher education at universities including prestigious ones such as Wuhan University and Xiamen University. These achievements came at the cost of Zhang's health.

"My colleagues and I almost gave up our lives in order to do it," she said. She's battling more than 10 diseases, such as emphysema and cerebellar atrophy, and six years ago, she stopped teaching due to poor health. Asked why she made so many efforts to help girls in the mountains receive better education, Zhang said she believes it is essential for girls to receive education as it will break the vicious circle between uneducated mothers and uneducated children. "Education for women can influence three generations of individuals," she said.

http://www.womenofchina.cn/womenofchina/html1/people/Inspiring/2007/6568-1.htm

Word Bank

inequality	*n.* the quality of being unequal or uneven 不平等
prejudice	*n.* an unreasonable dislike of a particular group of people or things, or a preference for one group of people or things over another 偏见
region	*n.* a large area of land that is different from other areas of land 地区，地带
extracurricular	*adj.* outside the regular academic curriculum 学校课程以外的，课外
inspire	*v.* heighten or intensify 激励；启发；赋予灵感；唤起（感情）；吸入（空气）
compulsory	*adj.* required by rule 强迫的；义务的；规定的
donate	*v.* give to a charity or good cause 赠送；捐献
humiliate	*v.* cause to feel shame; hurt the pride of 使蒙羞；屈辱，羞辱

representative	*adj.* serving to represent or typify 典型的；有代表性的
consequently	*adv.* as a consequence 因此；结果
allocate	*v.* distribute according to a plan or set apart for a special purpose 分配，分派
respectively	*adv.* in the order given 各自地；各个地
ensure	*v.* make certain of 确保；担保
initial	*adj.* occurring at the beginning 开始的
enroll	*v.* register formally as a participant or member 注册；登记；招收
humble	*adj.* cause to be unpretentious 谦逊的；简陋的
paralyze	*v.* make powerless and unable to function 使瘫痪，使麻痹
dishearten	*v.* take away the enthusiasm of 使失去勇气，使失去信心
handover	*n.* act of relinquishing property or authority 移交；交接
prestigious	*adj.* having an illustrious reputation; respected 受尊敬的，有声望的
emphysema	*n.* an abnormal condition of the lungs marked by decreased respiratory function 肺气肿
cerebellar atrophy	［医］小脑萎缩
vicious	*adj.* (of persons or their actions) able or disposed to inflict pain or suffering 邪恶的，恶毒的

Task 1 *Read the article and pick up the best choice.*

1. Why is the Huaping High School for Girls well-known in China?

    A) Because it is a girls' public high school.

    B) Because it does not charge tuition fees.

    C) Because it has high graduation rate.

    D) Because Zhang Guimei is teaching there.

2. Which of the following statements is TRUE about Zhang Guimei?

    A) She was appointed the headmaster of the Huaping High School in 2001.

    B) She was supported by local people and get money to build up a school.

    C) She was diagnosed cancer so she stopped teaching.

    D) She was selected as a representative of the 17th CPC National Congress in 2007.

3. Why did the mother in Para. 4 send her son to an extracurricular training institution instead of her daughter?

    A) Because she could not afford it.

    B) Because she thought it was more important for boys to study.

    C) Because her daughter was not willing to do that.

    D) Because people there never sent girls to school.

4. Why did Zhang Guimei make so many efforts to help girls in the mountains receive better education?

A) Education for women can boost economic development.

B) Education for women can change the condition of girls in rural areas.

C) Education for women can influence three generations of individuals.

D) Education for women can improve gender equality.

Task 2   *Please retell the following short paragraph by using your own words.*

Disheartened by the reality, Zhang also prepared for the handover. As she was organizing the documents, she found six out of the eight remaining staff workers at the school were members of the Communist Party of China. Zhang gathered them and they reviewed the oath of joining the Party together in front of a Party flag they drew. Everyone burst into tears before they could finish the oath.

Task 3   *Please share ideas with your partners about the following questions based on what you have read.*

1. Who is Zhang Guimei?

2. What contributions has Zhang made for the girls' education in the mountainous regions in Yunnan Province?

3. Why do we need people like Zhang Guimei in the process of rural revitalization?

4. What spirit do you learn from Zhang Guimei and her colleagues?

Task 4   *Work with your partners to fill the timeline below, and then retell Zhang Guimei's deeds in your own words according to the timeline.*

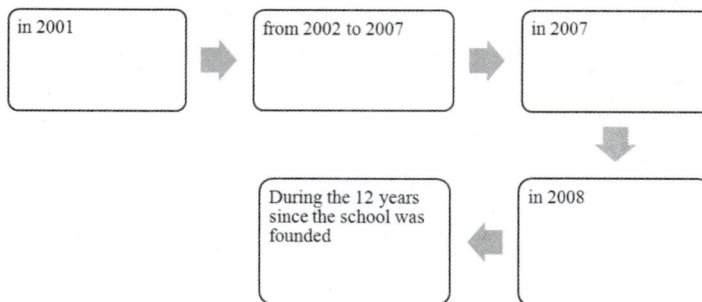

in 2001	→	from 2002 to 2007	→	in 2007
				↓
		During the 12 years since the school was founded	←	in 2008

IELTS Speaking Skill — Expressing Agreement and Disagreement

It is very common that one needs to express agreement or disagreement towards other's opinions or claims about some specific topics given. You can use the following expressions when agreeing or disagreeing with others.

Expressing agreement

I couldn't agree with you more.

That's so true.

That's for sure.

(slang) Tell me about it!

You're absolutely right.

Absolutely.

That's exactly how I feel.

Exactly.

I'm afraid I agree with James.

I have to side with Dad on this one.

No doubt about it.

You have a point here.

I was just going to say that.

Disagreeing politely

Whenever you show your different points in discussion, please remember that you have to be polite because you respect your partners, and want your discussion continue in a friendly atmosphere.

I'm sorry I have a different idea.

I'm afraid I can't agree with you.

I see your point, but ...

I think you're right about A, but I don't agree with you on B.

That may be true, but ...

That's an interesting idea/point, but ...

You may be right, but I tend to think ... /I want to stress ... /I want to emphasize ...

/I'd like to highlight ...

Yes, but don't you think ...
I'd say the exact opposite.

Task 1   *The following items contain important vocabulary from the listening material about Tu Youyou. Work with a partner and match vocabulary terms with their definitions. Check your answers in a dictionary if necessary.*

_____ 1. For decades, she worked almost **anonymously** before winning the Nobel Prize in 2015.

_____ 2. Through research, I find that Chinese medicine and western medicine each has its own advantages and can be **complementary** to each other.

_____ 3. The researcher and her team helped **isolate** an anti-malaria medicine inspired by an ancient, traditional remedy.

_____ 4. The discovery of Artemisinin has led to development of a new drug that has saved the lives of millions of people, **halving** the mortality rate of malaria during the past 15 years.

_____ 5. Your discoveries represent a **paradigm** shift in medicine, ...

_____ 6. ... which has not only provided revolutionary therapies for patients suffering from **devastating** parasitic diseases ...

_____ 7. I was impressed by her **persistence** in her work and scientific research...

_____ 8. I should learn from her **down-to-earth** method.

_____ 9. But she didn't rest on her **laurels** after winning these awards.

_____ 10. ... her team has **proposed** solutions to the problem of artemisinin resistance...

a. the property of a continuous and connected period of time

b. to make a proposal, declare a plan for something

c. to overwhelm or overpower

d. to divide into halve

e. acting as or providing a complement

f. to set apart from others

g. without giving a name

h. a standard or typical example

i. success

j. sensible and practical

Task 2 *Listen to the audio about Tu Youyou and pick up the best choice.*

1. What did Tu Youyou win the 2015 Nobel Prize for?

   A) The discovery of a drug that is now the top treatment for pneumonia.

   B) The discovery of an effective treatment for depression.

   C) The discovery of artemisinin, a drug that is effective for malaria.

   D) The discovery of artemisinin, a drug that is now the top treatment for malaria.

2. How many traditional Chinese medicines did Tu Youyou experiment?

   A) About 380.   B) Over 200.

   C) About 191.   D) More than 380.

3. Which of the following is TRUE about Tu Youyou?

   A) She suffered from a lung disease when she was young.

   B) She tested the medicine on her own without knowing by others.

   C) She started her work at Chinese Herbal Medicine Group.

   D) She isolated an anti-malaria medicine inspired by an ancient, traditional remedy.

4. What is the significance of Tu Youyou's work?

   A) Her work helped isolate an anti-malaria medicine inspired by an ancient, traditional remedy.

   B) Her work has led to development of a new drug that has saved the lives of millions of people.

   C) Her work has helped significantly reduce the mortality rates of malaria patients.

   D) Her work proved that ancient Chinese medicine has valuable treasure.

5. What did Dr. Ma Yue say about Tu Youyou?

   A) She said Tu looks a little bit serious.

   B) She said she should learn from her teacher.

   C) She said Tu's students impressed her a lot.

   D) She said Tu was the greatest scientist in her mind.

Task 3 *Listen to the audio again and fill the following blanks according what you hear.*

1. Tu Youyou won the 2015 Nobel Prize for the discovery of artemisinin, a drug that is now the _____. Tu has risked her life in her dedication to _____.

2. We should work hard to _____ the rich resources in it. Artemisinin was discovered from it. Through research, I find that Chinese medicine and western medicine each has its own advantages and _____.

3. The researcher and her team helped _____ an anti-malaria medicine inspired

by an _____. The discovery of artemisinin has helped significantly _____ of malaria patients.

4. Your discoveries represent a _____ in medicine, which has not only provided _____ for patients suffering from _____, but also promoted well-being and prosperity for individuals and society.

5. I experimented on over 200 kinds of Chinese medicines and I tried about _____ _____ in total. They all failed. I named my starting point as No.91, because I found the _____ after 191 experiments.

6. Tu Youyou also won China's top science award in 2017 for her outstanding contributions to _____. But she didn't _____ after winning these awards. She continued to work at perfecting her discoveries.

Task 4   *Please share ideas with your partners about the following questions.*

1. Can you list more scientists who share the same quality or spirit of Tu Youyou? Illustrate one of them.

2. What is the connotation of "spirit of scientists"? Can you explain by giving examples?

Task 5   *Make a conversation with your partners about one of the following topics. Try to use expressions of agreement/disagreement discussed in the previous part. You can do peer or self-evaluation by using the criteria below.*

1. Our government should give more support to the development of traditional Chinese medicine.

2. Everyone should learn some knowledge about traditional Chinese medicine in order to be healthy.

3. We should take the road of integration of traditional Chinese and Western medicine, especially after the test of anti-COVID-19 battle.

Criteria for Peer- / Self-Assessment

NO.	Analytic Items	Proportion	Peer- /Self-Assessment
1	Using expressions of agreement and disagreement properly	20%	
2	Fluency (less accidental pauses, short pause length, less self-correction)	20%	
3	Accuracy (accuracy in using words and expressions, accuracy in grammar use)	20%	
4	Complexity(lexical variety, usage of less frequent vocabulary, syntactic complexity)	20%	
5	Pronunciation (no strong accent, correct stress, liaison, plosion in words and sentences, sounds naturally)	20%	
Total Score (use a 10-point scale)			

Part Five   Critical Thinking

Li Ziqi, a Celebrity as an Ambassador of Chinese Culture

Guinness World Records announced through its official micro blog account that livestreaming star Li Ziqi had, with 14.1 million followers, beaten her own earlier record as the person with the most followers on the Chinese YouTube channel. Though she features on YouTube's Chinese channel, her appeal knows no boundaries, with viewers around the world commenting favorably under her videos.

Born in a remote countryside of Sichuan Province in 1990, Li was raised by her grandmother and went out to make a living at her teens. After many twists and turns, she finally came back home to look after her sick grandmother, and took the production

新理念雅思口语教程
A Transformative Course Book: IELTS Speaking

of short videos as her job. In her videos, she makes everything and grow everything by herself. She seems to be a master of all kinds of skills, cooking, painting, farming and designing.

What's the secret behind Li's mass appeal? The answer lies in her style and content. Instead of preaching to her audiences, Li tells her story as it is, like, say, about growing beans, harvesting them, grinding them into powder and fermenting it to make bean sauce. In another video Li shows how to make traditional Chinese ink, starting by burning wood, collecting the smoke, adding water to make a black paste and lastly using the handmade paste to draw on bamboos in the traditional Chinese way. That way she also ends up promoting traditional Chinese culture before a global audience.

In 2017, Li released her first video on YouTube explaining how to dye a dress using the skins of grapes. She went viral overseas afterward with her short videos about cooking Chinese food, making traditional Chinese handicrafts such as embroidery and living an idyllic rural life in China. Experts say she successfully teaches people to appreciate Chinese culture around the world.

Unlike other popular short videos, each of Li's videos usually lasts 10 minutes, recording an elaborate process of meal preparation from cultivating the basic ingredients to sharing the food with her grandmother in the backyard, and some handicrafts, like the China's "scholar's four jewels," — namely the writing brush, ink stick, ink slab and paper. In most of her videos, she seldom speaks but simply shows the way she relishes her idyllic life with her grandmother, with traditional Chinese music and natural sounds playing in the background. The backdrops are usually the backyard of her house or extensive mountains and clear waters, where she mostly wears traditional Han costumes and use the simplest tools to make food. The perfect fusion of makeup, image and sound stands in stark contrast to other more popular videos.

The idyllic setting and lifestyle also cast doubts as to whether she is portraying Chinese rural life authentically. Some hold the opinion that what Ziqi displays in her videos is an ideal that people are seeking after. Scenes of the young vlogger picking seasonal ingredients from her own garden (and sometimes in the mountains and rivers near her residence) and turning them into luscious dishes on her wood-fired wok dominate her videos. A warm bowl of soup for the winter, a lighter plate of noodles for the summer. Li emphasizes the seasons in her cooking, as China's traditional 24 Solar Terms also do, and makes food suitable for the particular climate.

One of her fans comments, "Watching her videos, it is difficult not to appreciate their beauty and hold back that sense of nostalgia and longing for home. But it is even harder to not want to take a bite of her succulent dishes."

"I'm filming myself. Or I'm filming the life that I am pursuing," Ziqi said in the interview and admitted that professional videographers were involved but added they were all directed by her.

"China has tried for so many years to promote our culture globally but made little progress, and that's because of a lack of spontaneity and focus on Chinese people's daily lives," Zhang Xiaoming, director of the China National Center for Culture Studies under the Chinese Academy of Social Sciences, said in a recent interview with The Beijing News. "China needs more Li Ziqi". Cultural promotion via official way and civil recreational channels are equally important. We need to present good stories about China from multiple dimensions.

However, what she promotes is often a legacy of the past; China is no longer how she depicts it in her videos. Chinese farmers now harvest crops with machines, not with hands, and have long been cooking with natural gas, instead of using wood. All the progress that technology can bring has reached China, with 37,900 kilometers of high-speed railways, about 70 percent of the world's total, and 989 million internet users.

It is time for more Chinese individuals and media to learn from Li and draw a fuller portrait of modern China before the world.

Adapted from the article from https://mp.weixin.qq.com/s/CXMyuVorMdiz8nqkTPxWeA

Task 1 *Read the article and summarize what makes Li's videos gain such a great popularity online. You should add details to support. You may jot down the key points in the following box.*

Tell your partners do you agree or disagree to the following statements, and give reasons to support your idea.

Statement one: Li is NOT portraying Chinese rural life authentically. But she provides people in modern society with an opportunity to escape from skullduggeries and seek for peaceful mind.

The reason:

Statement two: Li Ziqi can be regarded as an Ambassador of Chinese Culture. And there should be more celebrities like her to promote our traditional culture and current achievements to the outside world.

The reason:

Task 3 *Listen to the story about Lang Lang, the famous pianist, and fill in the following blanks.*

1. Lang Lang is one of the world's _____. His _____ was when he was just two years old.

2. Neighbors would often _____ his door and ask him to stop practicing. They were so angry that he often feared that they would _____.

3. One afternoon, his teacher told him he had no talent and told him to go home. Upon

hearing the news, his father _____ and seemed to _____.

4. Finally, when he was 10, he was accepted into the Central Conservatory of Music with _____. In 1995, when he was 13 years old, he played music by Chopin in _____.

5. One American _____ called him "the biggest, most exciting keyboard talent I have _____ in many a year of attending piano recitals."

6. And in the end, Lang Lang and his father have _____. In his autobiography, Mr. Lang _____ his mother and father.

Task 4   *Listen to the above story again and choose the best answer according to what you hear.*

1. Which of the following is true about Lang Lang?

   A) He first contact with Chinese music when he was two.

   B) He won his first place in a piano competition when he was three.

   C) He left his mother to study in Beijing when he was nine.

   D) He studied in the Central Conservatory of Music when he was nine.

2. Why did the neighbors feel angry?

   A) Because they have no money for paying for the rent.

   B) Because Lang Lang's practice disturbed their neighbors.

   C) Because the father of Lang Lang is bad-tempered.

   D) Because Lang Lang's father always shouted on Lang Lang.

3. Why did Lang Lang play piano again after he had a conflict with his father?

   A) Because his father apologized to him.

   B) Because his teacher spurred him.

   C) Because his mother comfort him.

   D) Because his friends encouraged him.

4. When did Lang Lang become a major star?

   A) After he studied with a famous pianist in America.

   B) When he was 13 years old.

   C) When he was accepted into the Conservatory.

   D) When he won an international competition in Japan.

Task 5   *Please discuss with your partners about the following questions.*

1. What makes Lang Lang successful and prestigious? Illustrate them.

2. Do you think Lang Lang had the same ups and downs of being a celebrity mentioned in the previous task? Why?

3. What kind of celebrities, in your mind, are deserved to be idols of the youngsters?

4. What do you think about the relationship between Lang Lang and his father?

Task 6   *Please share your idea with your partners about one of the following statements.*

1. Do not, for one repulse, give up the purpose that you resolved to effect.

2. Genius only means hard-working all one's life.

3. Our destiny offers not the cup of despair, but the chalice of opportunity.

4. The important thing in life is to have a great aim, and the determination to attain it.

5. The only limit to our realization of tomorrow will be our doubts of today.

6. A strong man will struggle with the storms of fate.

7. Energy and persistence conquer all things.

8. Try not to become a man of success but rather try to become a man of value.

Part Six   Encountering IELTS Speaking

Words and Expressions about Persons

alert 敏捷机灵的

ambitious 有雄心的

amiable 和蔼可亲的

analytical 善于分析的

apprehensive 有理解力的

aspiring 有抱负的

diligent 勤奋的

conscientious 勤奋敬业的

enthusiastic 热情的

versatile 多才多艺的

talented/gifted 有才华的

intelligent 聪明的

witty 风趣的

quick-witted 机智的，反应快的

resourceful 深谋远虑的，足智多谋的

considerate 体贴的

dependable 可靠的

diplomatic 老练的

discreet 小心谨慎的

double eyelid 双眼皮

energetic 精力充沛的

expressive 善于表达的

faithful 忠诚的

forceful 有说服力的

frank 直率的

generous 宽宏大量的

gentle 有礼貌的

hard-working 勤劳的

hearty 亲切的

hospitable 好客的

humorous 幽默的

independent 有主见的

industrious 勤奋的

confident/assertive 自信的

bubbly 活泼的

carefree 无忧无虑的

optimistic 乐观的

pessimistic 悲观的

well-mannered 有礼貌的

urbane 温文尔雅的，斯文的

a man of stout build 矮胖的人

a short person 矮个子

about/around 40 大约 40 岁

in his/her 30's 在他 / 她 30 多岁时

medium height 中等身高

average height 一般身高

middle-sized 身高中等的

below average 低于平均身高

tallish 有些高的

overweight 超重

slight 瘦小的

shapely 身材匀称的

dashing 精神抖擞的

dazzling 耀眼的

stunning 极好的

hunky 健美有魅力

delicate 精致的

charming 迷人的

neat 整洁的

oval face 瓜子脸

overweight 偏胖的

plait 编的辫子

plump 丰满的

plump/chubby cheeks 胖胖的脸蛋

pointed chin 尖下巴

round face 圆脸

slight of figure 身材瘦小的

gentle and graceful （女性）窈窕的

slim 苗条的

square face 方脸

wavy hair 波浪形头发

well made-up 化妆的

well-built （男性）健壮的

with wrinkles/lines 有皱纹的

gorgeous 长相完美

average / plain / common looking 长相一般

good looking 长得好看

fair-skinned 皮肤白皙的

full lips 厚嘴唇

a pale complexion 肤色暗淡的

oval face 瓜子脸

slightly dark / tanned 肤色较深

square face 方脸

publisher 出版人员

graphic designer 美术设计员

journalist 记者

editor 编辑

interpreter 口译者

director 导演

talent 星探

actor 男演员

actress 女演员

photographer 摄影师

producer 制片人

scholar 学者

translator 翻译家

novelist 小说家

playwright 剧作家

linguist 语言学家

botanist 植物学家

economist 经济学家

chemist 化学家

scientist 科学家

philosopher 哲学家

politician 政治学家

physicist 物理学家

anthropologist 人类学家

archaeologist 考古学家

geologist 地质学家

expert on folklore 民俗学家

mathematician 数学家

biologist 生物学家

zoologist 动物学家

statistician 统计学家

physiologist 生理学家

geologist 地质学家

extroverted/sociable/outgoing 外向的

introverted/shy 内向的

frugal 节俭的

dashing 有闯劲的

snobbish 势力的

aggressive 霸道的

cheeky 厚颜无耻的

stubborn 顽固的

hypocritical 虚伪的

self-conceited 自负的

self-centered 自私的

smug 沾沾自喜的，自满的

big-headed 妄自尊大的

pushy 坚持己见的

bossy 跋扈的

mediocre 平庸的

level-headed 遇事冷静的

forward-looking 有远见的

materialistic 过于现实的

mild 温和的

sympathetic 富有同情心的

compassionate 有爱心的

sincere 真诚的

honest 诚实的

trustworthy 可信赖的

candid 直率的

modest 谦逊的

arrogant 傲慢的

humorous 幽默的

funky 时髦的；古灵精怪的

sensitive 感性的

sensible 理性的

conservative 保守的

open-minded 开明的

careless 粗心大意的

generous 慷慨的

knowledgeable 有见地的，渊博的

tough/tenacious 顽强的

original 有原创性的

classy 很有品位的

punctual 守时的

oriental 黄皮肤的，东方人的

a haggard face 瘦削的脸

suntanned 棕褐色

baby-faced 娃娃脸

brown 棕色皮肤

chubby cheeks 胖乎乎的脸

pale 肤色苍白

high-bridged nose 高鼻梁

long nose 长鼻梁

noble nose 好看的鼻子

flat nose 塌鼻

snub-nosed 朝天鼻

aquiline / hooked nose 鹰钩鼻

a roman nose 鹰钩鼻，高鼻梁
bald 光秃的
beard 络腮胡
moustache 唇上的胡子
broad-shouldered 宽肩的
clean-shaven 刮过脸的
long eye lashes 长睫毛
thin lips 薄嘴唇
straight nose 直鼻梁
thick lips 厚嘴唇
cherry lips 樱桃嘴
straight 直的
dyed 染色的
curly 卷发的
golden 金黄色的
wavy hair 波浪发
jet-black 乌黑的
spiky hair 刺头，板寸头
blonde 淡黄色（金发美女）
crew cut 平头
blond 淡黄的（金发男）
bald 秃头的
fair 金色的
pigtails 辫子
brunette 浅黑色的
parted hair 分头
mousey 灰褐色的
chestnut 栗色的
fashion coordinator 时装搭配师
dressmaker 女装裁剪师

cutter 裁剪师
sewer 裁缝师
tailor 西装师傅
beautician 美容师
model 模特
ballerina 芭蕾舞者
detective 刑警
fire fighter 消防人员
chief of police 警察局长
car mechanic 汽车修理师
architect 建筑师
civil planner 城市设计师
civil engineer 土木技师
druggist, chemist, pharmacist 药剂师
guide 导游
oil supplier 加油工
(public) health nurse 保健护士
dentist 牙科医生
national public servant 国家公务员
local public service employee 地方公务员
gas station attendant 加油工
futurologist 未来学家
artist 艺术家
painter 画家
musician 音乐家
composer 作曲家
designer 设计家
sculptor 雕刻家
designer 服装设计师

IELTS Speaking Skill — Lexical Resource

Lexical resource refers to the range of vocabulary which you use accurately for conveying your intended meaning. The wider you range, the higher you score. In order to achieve Band 7, you should:

- uses vocabulary resource flexibly to discuss a variety of topics
- uses some less common and idiomatic vocabulary and shows some awareness of style and collocation, with some inappropriate choices
- uses paraphrase effectively

How to build vocabulary for IELTS Speaking?

- Collocation — words that go together

  He is a heavy sleeper.

  He threw a party last Friday.
- Phrasal verbs — verb + preposition

  Switch on the light.

  He looks down on poor people.
- Less common idioms — simple expressions but difficult for non-native speakers to understand

  I have a lot on my plate. (I'm very busy.)

  I go to movies once in a blue moon. (very rarely)
- Paraphrase — use different words to express the same idea, usually to make it shorter or clearer

  I usually end my day by drinking some coffee.

  I take a sip of coffee and then turn in.

You may refer to the Table 4–1 for more details.

Table 4–1　IELTS Speaking Test Band Descriptors of Grammar

Band	Descriptor of Lexical Resource
9	- uses vocabulary with full flexibility and precision in all topics - uses idiomatic language naturally and accurately
8	- uses a wide vocabulary resource readily and flexibly to convey precise meaning - uses less common and idiomatic vocabulary skillfully, with occasional inaccuracies - uses paraphrase effectively as required
7	- uses vocabulary resource flexibly to discuss a variety of topics - uses some less common and idiomatic vocabulary and shows some awareness of style and collocation, with some inappropriate choices - uses paraphrase effectively

Band	Descriptor of Lexical Resource
6	■ has a wide enough vocabulary to discuss topics at length and make meaning clear in spite of inappropriacies ■ generally paraphrases successfully
5	■ manages to talk about familiar and unfamiliar topics but uses vocabulary with limited flexibility ■ attempts to use paraphrase but with mixed success

Task 1   *Please describe the famous Chinese sprinter Su Bingtian who performed marvelously in the 2020 Tokyo Olympic Games by considering the criteria of lexical resource. You can refer to the following outline.*

His outer appearance

His performance in the 2020 Tokyo Olympic Games

The comments from media and audience

Your own feeling towards him

Task 2 *Please describe one of our alumni you admire by considering the criteria of lexical resource. You can refer to the following outline.*

Who he/she is

Which department did he/he graduate

What did he/she do

What you can learn from him/her

IELTS Speaking Test items

Part 1

1. What are the qualities of a good teacher?
2. Do you think you could be a teacher?
3. What makes a good teacher?
4. Do you have any friends who live far away from you?
5. What do you value most in friends?
6. Do you have many friends?
7. How do you make friends?
8. Do you like chatting with friends?
9. Would you like to be a celebrity in the future?
10. What kinds of people become famous?

1. What are the qualities of a good teacher?

I get along well with those teachers who are friendly, patient and have a good sense of humor. I mean, I am quite sensitive. My teacher's attitude can affect me a lot. Also, it's important that the teacher knows how to guide me and is able to engage us.

2. Do you think you could be a teacher?

I don't think I am suitable to be a teacher, I am not a patient man and cannot bear to repeat the same things frequently. Teachers' job is really boring to me, you have to make your explanations as easy as possible for students to fully understand. It is a challenging job, I am afraid I cannot do it.

3. What makes s good teacher?

I should say a good teacher is one who always is well prepared for the class. And I guess if the person has a good sense of humor that would help because, you know, boring, ah, session, nobody would sit in the class, you know, hours after hours.

Part 2

1. Describe a famous foreigner you particularly admire.

You should say:

Who this person is;

Why he/she is famous;

Why you admire him/her;

And explain how he/she contributes to society.

▶ Sample Answer

Talking about a famous foreigner, I want to talk about David Beckham, one of the most famous football players in the world. He's extremely well-known, and I believe that everyone around the world could recognize him if they saw him on TV or in a newspaper.

First of all, in the 1990s, Beckham used to be a very successful athlete. He used to play for Manchester United, and he won the Premier League 6 times with this club. They even won the European Champions League, which is the most prestigious club competition in the world. Everyone praised his ability to kick the ball and deliver amazing passes. Goalkeepers always feared his free kicks, and he even played for AC Milan, which is one of the strongest teams in Europe. A movie entitled *Bend it like Beckham* was even made. He is a role model for many young people.

Beckham got married to a former band member of the famous "Spice Girls". His wife's name is Victoria and she is an attractive singer who somehow managed to bring Beckham to another level of fame. The two of them are the constant center of attention of the press. Paparazzis follow them on a daily basis, and I believe that there is not a day without an article published about Beckham and his wife. They seem so happy. You know, so many celebrities divorce, but they've been together for a long time and have several cute children.

I think that his wife played a major role in his career. David is a good-looking man, and he learned how to make full use of his name and appearance. Beckham advertises for many famous brands. He models, he acts, he publishes books, too. In 2002, he launched his debut book named *My side*, which was a really hit! He's a real successful man.

2. Describe an adventurous person you know.
   You should say:
   Who this person is;
   How you know this person;
   What kind of person he/she is;
   And explain why you think he/she is adventurous.

▶ **Sample Answer**
   Talking about an adventurous person, I want to talk about Jack. He works as an engineer for a company in Jiangsu Province.

   I met him while I was travelling in Guilin during my summer vacation in my first year of high school. He was riding a tricycle and carrying a small bike at the same time, which impressed me a lot. I made a compliment and he laughed about it. And then, we started to chat as it turned out we were both looking for a place to stay. So, we chatted and wandered until we found a decent youth hostel.

Jack told me that he was really into cycling and spent a large amount of his free time travelling to various places to cycle and sightseeing at the same time. We decided to go cycling the next day together. We went out of town and started up cycling in a narrow path beside a river with rolling fields off to the other side. Although the place was so tranquil and picturesque, I found it quite hard to cycle and almost fell into the river at one point. However, Jack was experienced and kindly slowed down so that I could keep up. He told me that he had cycled in much more difficult conditions where the terrain was steeper and more rugged.

I guess he is so adventurous because he loves the thrill of exploring new places. I suppose he's a bit of adrenaline junkie, but at the same time he has a very calm disposition. He told me he could get a huge sense of achievement and satisfaction when he cycled in such exciting places.

3. Describe a teacher you have had.
   You should say:
   Who the teacher is;
   What the teacher is like;
   How he/she taught;
   And explain what effect the teacher had on you.

   ▶ **Sample Answer**
   Talking about teachers in my life, I would like to mention Mr. Li who was my physics teacher at middle school in Shanghai. He is so important for me because he provided not only education but more critically, life guidance.

   Mr. Li had his own way of teaching and seemed interested in all the members of the class — the weaker students as well as the clever ones, which really impressed me. And he also had a good sense of humor. I thought physics could be pretty boring sometimes, but when he found we'd stopped paying attention, he'd tell us a quick joke, and that would wake us up and he could go on with the lesson. His teaching methodology was so versatile that we never felt bored. It was so fun!

Most importantly, he helped us learn what learning was all about. He taught us not only a subject, but also how to carry on learning about the subject after class. For example, he said that we should always try to keep an enquiring and open mind; physics wasn't just a subject in textbook; it was a way of looking at the world and it could help us to understand the way in which the world worked. And many of us have benefited from this quite a lot because it changed our way of learning. I will always thank him for his devoted guide.

As the saying goes, "A mediocre teacher tells; a good teacher explains; a superior teacher demonstrates; and a great teacher inspires." To me, he is the greatest teacher I have ever known.

4. Describe a member of your family who you are very close to.
   You should say:
   Who the family member is;
   How you are like that family member;
   How you differ from the family member;
   And explain why you are close to him/her.

5. Describe a happy person you know.
   You should say:
   Who the person is;
   How you came to know him/her;
   Whether you know him/her well;
   And explain what makes this person such a happy person.

Part 3

1. Which type of people are respected most in our society?

2. What happens when young people lack good role models?

3. What standards of behavior should teachers set?

4. What can parents do to give children correct guidance?

5. In your culture, what kinds of people can be leaders?

6. Has there been a change in the characteristics that leaders should have?

7. Many women are earning more money now; does it mean that they can be larders?

8. Would you want to be famous in the future?

9. Do you think we should protect celebrities' privacy?

10. Why do some young people want to be famous?

11. What do you think of fame?

12. Do you think celebrities' wrong behaviors will have a bad influence on young people?

13. How do people become famous in your country?

14. Why do some famous people do bad things?

15. What is the reason that movie stars earn more than nurses?

▶ **Sample Answer**

1. Which type of people are respected most in our society?

   I think that generally, the type of people that others look up to are mainly those with money and very expensive possessions. Like those who have homes that are lavish, luxury cars and designer clothes. Others may have more respect for those who do jobs that are difficult and rewarding, for example, doctors, nurses and teachers. Speaking for myself, I would say that I hold those in high regard who work for non-profit organizations, helping those who have nothing, like the homeless, refugees and animal shelters.

2. What happens when young people lack good role models?

   In my view, they can become difficult and have no direction in life. Without someone to look up to, they have no one to follow, to show them right from wrong and how to have a good life. Impressionable young people will then follow someone with a strong personality, even though they might not be the best example.

新理念雅思口语教程
A Transformative Course Book: IELTS Speaking

3. What standards of behavior should teachers set?

When students are in school, the teacher should be an exemplary role model for them to follow. They spend so much time with their teachers during this time that the lessons they learn and the behaviors they see, will shape their own behaviors. For example, the teacher will create classroom rules that all students have to follow. In my view, this is a good example of the teacher being a strong person that the students should look up to.

Checklist for This Chapter

Please check according to the scale from 1 to 5.

(1 — Strongly Disagree; 2 — Disagree; 3 — Undecided; 4 —Agree; 5 — Strongly Agree)

Can-do List	1	2	3	4	5
I know how to describe people.					
I know how to summarize people's deeds chronologically.					
I know how to express agreement and disagreement.					
I know the value of selfless dedication and the qualities leading to success.					

Self-reflection

1. In which part have I done very well?

2. In which part should I make improvement?

3. What should I do to bridge the current gap?

4. What suggestions do I have for my teacher or the class arrangement?

5. Anything I would like to say.

(Your reflection could be written in Chinese)

Travel and Transport

LEARNING OBJECTIVES

In this chapter you will learn

- words and expressions about travel and transport in IELTS Speaking Test
- how to talk about places/travelling
- how to construct complex sentences
- how to use classification expressions to organize ideas
- the brilliant transport technology in China

Part One   Warming-up

Task 1   *What are different ways of travelling? Write down what you know about it (the first one has been done for you).*

NO.	Ways of Travelling	Features
1	airplane	expensive, fast, long travel distance to the airport
2	metro/subway	
3	cycle	
4	bus	
5	taxi	

Write down the key words for your answers.

1. What is your favourite way of travelling? Why is that?

_____

_____

2. What is the place you would like to visit most in the future? Why is that?

_____

_____

Task 3 *Work with your partner and write down the English expressions people often use to talk about travelling or transportation.*

1. 开拓我们的思维 _____

2. 开阔我们的眼界 _____

3. 离开繁忙的都市生活 _____

4. 暂时忘掉工作 _____

5. 我的（旅行）预算有限。 My _____ is very _____.

6. 堵在路上 _____

7. 这很难找到停车位。 It's _____.

8. （酒店等）位置非常方便，价格合理 _____

9. 离……只有几分钟的步行距离 _____

10. （建筑的）内部和外部 _____

11. 状况良好（老建筑或旧物品） _____

12. 它是我们文化遗产的重要部分。 It's an _____.

13. 值得参观 _____

14. 美化市容 _____

Part Two   IELTS Speaking Test

Talking about（Visiting）Places

In IELTS Speaking Test, you will often be asked to talk about places where you stay or you have visited before or want to visit in the future. You might also be asked about your experience or plans of visiting these places, e.g., a trip to a well-known place or travelling abroad. The following are examples of some possible topics.

> your apartment (or a room in your apartment) or your ideal house
> a public place (e.g. a library, a museum, a restaurant, a shopping center, a garden or a park, historic buildings)
> your home town
> a city or town that you have visited
> a trip you had with your friend
> a trip you took when you were a child

- **Expressions used to talk about a building/place**
  Notes: Descriptions can be approached from different aspects: the interior and exterior of a building; location & distance; feature & feeling, etc. For example,
  It's very *bright* inside _____. (**Interior**)
  You'll feel it's very *spacious* on the first floor. (**Interior**)
  The decoration is very modern because it's tailored for young people. (**Interior**)
  If you *look from the outside* and the whole building *is made of* glass and steel. (**Exterior**)
  From the outside, the Shangri-La Hotel is a *modern skyscraper*. (**Exterior**)
  The library *is situated* in the center of the campus.... (**Location**)
  The coffee house *is located on* a quiet street with a lot of trees planted on both sides. (**Location**)
  It is *on the opposite side* of my university. (**Location**)
  It is not very far from a subway station. (**Distance**)
  It's *within walking distance.* (**Distance**)
  It's *about 10 minutes' walk.* (**Distance**)
  It's *about 2 hours' drive.* (**Distance**)
  The museum is so *interesting and unique.* (**Feature**)

You *have enough space to stretch your arms and legs.* (**Feature**)

(The building) It's *been there for* about ten years. (**Feature**)

It can make people feel *happy and peaceful.* (**Feelings**)

It has given me *a lot of fun and enjoyment.* (**Feelings**)

It's *really not that enjoyable* if you live in the downtown area. (**Feelings**)

- **Talking about your home town or a city**

Information that can be included: what kind of place it is (general introduction: big city, or small town); what it is famous for; what you like/dislike about it; how it has changed over time, etc. For example,

I live in Shanghai. It's a huge, bustling, international city. People from all over the world live and work there. (*general introduction*)

Shanghai's a great place to live. It's a real 24-hour city and you can meet people from all over the world. (*what you like about the city*)

Shanghai's an exciting place, but it's really crowded and it can be exhausting to live there. Air quality can be an issue, particularly in the summer. (*what you dislike about the city*)

Shanghai is almost unrecognizable compared to twenty or thirty years ago. The city has expanded so much, both physically and economically. It's amazing when you see old photos of the city; things are so different now! (*talking about changes*)

- **Expressions used to talk about travelling experience or memory**

① Introducing your topic

This topic *reminds me of the trip to* _____ *with* _____ last year.

I *like travelling and I've been to many places. I remember* _____.

I still *remember the trip with* _____ *to* _____ *in* _____ *when I was* ____.

② Using descriptive words

The trip is *amazing, wonderful, unforgettable, memorable, disappointing ...*

The place is *interesting, beautiful, picturesque, spectacular, a must-see, ...*

We all felt *excited, exhausted, disappointed, ...*

Task 1 *Pair work. Please talk about your own home town with your partner. You can jot down the key words in the following box.*

```




```

Task 2 *Pair work. What is your favorite place on campus or near your neighborhood? Can you describe it?*

1.

2.

3.

Part Three   Speaking after Reading

The Ultimate Guide for a Successful Road Trip

With the changing situation around restrictions and lockdown, many travel plans have been put on hold, but, if you are lucky enough to get away, a UK road trip is a favorable option. Although the pandemic has changed travel as we know it, the road trip may be the least affected mode of transport, with minimal contact and interaction with other travelers needed.

From booking in advance to making sure you are safely social distancing, what needs to be considered in order to have a smooth road trip? Here, we have come up with some helpful tips ahead of going away by car, in the near or distant future.

Plan, plan, plan

Planning your trip is the key to staying safe and having fun. With travel restrictions changing at a quick pace, it may make it harder to plan well in advance, but it is extremely important to do so nonetheless.

For the trip itself, plan your itinerary clearly, making sure to do your research to check that landmarks and areas of interest are operating. While you can socialize within your own small travel group, mixing with large groups of other travelers won't be possible. Restaurants, bars, and other events will be operating on a smaller, more restricted scale, so bear this in mind when making arrangements.

Remember to pack all the necessary equipment, such as masks, hand sanitizer, and anti-bacterial wipes, to ensure you are equipped to follow safety guidelines.

Expect it to get busier

Since there has been a rise in staycations in the UK, depending where you are going, you may experience more crowds than usual as well as a higher demand for hotels, landmarks, pubs, and other restaurants. Although this should not be an issue for many, if you are wanting a tranquil staycation, it may be worth tweaking where you go to avoid disappointment. For example, popular staycation resorts like Cornwall and The Lake District will inevitably be busy, while lesser known places like Durham and the Scottish Isles may not be. When considering a time of year for your trip, it is worth opting for autumn or spring months, purely for the vibrant colors during this period.

To avoid heavy traffic, opt to travel outside of peak times and weekends, as this may have a substantial impact on travel time. It is also worth buying and looking over road maps in advance as this is the best way to discover the roads worth driving as well as build excitement.

Pre-trip checks

When embarking on a long car journey, it is vital that your vehicle is in sound condition beforehand. Ahead of departure, conduct your regular checks by looking over the battery, tyres, and fluids to ensure everything is in order. Turn the engine on and assess the **dashboard** for any warning lights, taking the time to check all of the car's interior and exterior lighting is working.

In addition, make sure you have sufficient car insurance and road tax in place before taking your car out as you don't want this to expire mid-trip.

Fuel

Before setting off on a road trip, check you have sufficient fuel and even consider packing a spare tank, as it may be harder to find a petrol station, especially if you are off the beaten track. Depending where you are, you may find that fuel prices are more expensive in certain locations, so planning this efficiently ahead of time will ensure you get the best value. It is also worth noting that fuel prices tend to be slightly higher at service stations, so try your best to fuel up before.

Take regular breaks

On long road trips, driving for long periods of time can take its toll, even for experienced drivers. Drivers should ideally take a break every 2 hours and should incorporate stretching your legs and getting fresh air as part of this, to help avoid stiffness and drowsiness. Where possible avoid driving for long periods at night-time and try to diversify the scenery, as long straight roads are more likely to cause tiredness. It is also recommended to rotate drivers if possible, to give you the chance to relax.

Most importantly, have fun!

It's important to remember that no matter how much you plan you can never predict what will happen on the road. But by taking a few simple steps, you can make sure that your next road trip is a safe and successful one. You're on holiday after all, enjoy it!

Adapted from *Reader's Digest*

Word Bank

restriction	*adj.* a rule or law that limits what you can do or what can happen 限制规定
itinerary	*n.* a plan or line of travel; route 行程；路线
(hand) sanitizer	*n.* 洗手液；消毒剂
anti-bacterial	*adj.* a disinfectant 抗菌的
staycation	*n.* a vacation in which one does not travel away from home 居家度假
tranquil	*adj.* quiet and peaceful 平静的；恬静的
tweak	*v.* to make slight changes 稍微调整
opt (for)	*v.* to choose 选择
vibrant	*adj.* 有活力的
substantial	*adj.* large in amount, value or importance 巨大的
embark	*v.* start to do something new or difficult 开始；着手
off the beaten **track**	remote from populous or much-traveled regions 偏僻地
take its **toll**	cause a loss to 造成损失
stiffness	*n.* being difficult to bend or move 僵硬
drowsiness	*n.* sleepiness 困倦
diversify	*v.* to increase the variety of 使多样化

Task 1 *Read the article and choose the best answer.*

1. Which of the following is not mentioned by the author concerning going on a road trip?

   A) Make plans in advance.

   B) Save enough money for the trip.

   C) Check your car condition.

   D) Stop and stretch legs for long-time driving.

2. What does the author suggest for those who want to have a peaceful vacation?

   A) Pay attention to travel restrictions.

   B) Be willing to make slight changes about your destination.

   C) Buy road maps in advance.

   D) Stay safe and have fun.

3. What does **dashboard** probably mean in Line 4 of the part "**Pre-trip checks**"?

   A) The part of a car in front of the driver that has instruments and controls in it.

   B) The part of a car that a driver uses to accelerate a car.

   C) The part of a car that a driver uses to slow down a car.

   D) The part of a car that is used to improve the driver's safety.

4. In the part "**Take regular breaks**", which of the following is **NOT** mentioned?

    A) Switching drivers.

    B) Getting fresh air.

    C) Stretching your legs.

    D) Having a good sleep.

Task 2   *Please share ideas with your partner about the following questions based on what you read.*

1. Why does the author say planning the trip is the key to a smooth road trip?

2. Apart from what is discussed in the article, what else can you suggest for having a wonderful road trip in China?

3. How are you going to prepare for a road trip if one day your family will go vacation together?

4. What is the first thing on your priority list concerning a road trip? Why?

Task 3   *Please retell the following short paragraph using your own words.*

On long road trips, driving for long periods of time can take its toll, even for experienced drivers. Drivers should ideally take a break every 2 hours and should incorporate stretching your legs and getting fresh air as part of this, to help avoid stiffness and drowsiness. Where possible avoid driving for long periods at night-time and try to diversify the scenery, as long straight roads are more likely to cause tiredness. It is also recommended to rotate drivers if possible, to give you the chance to relax.

Task 4   *Pair work. Please discuss the following questions with your partner.*

1. Have you ever travelled by car before? What kind of experience was it?

2. What are the pros and cons of going on a road trip? Give detailed information based on the following points. Write down some key words to help you if necessary.

Reasons to Go on a Road Trip	Reasons to Think Twice about a Road Trip
You are in charge _____	Driving takes time _____
You can change your mind _____	You have to do all the work _____
You can see the real world _____	You have to park the car _____
You can pack anything that fits into your trunk _____	Travelling by car can be expensive _____
You can save money _____	Wear and tear on your car costs money _____
	You have to get back _____

Part Four   Speaking after Listening

IELTS Speaking Skill — Organizing Your thoughts

When giving a long and detailed answer, it would be easier if you can follow some ways to organize your thoughts. The following methods and expressions can be helpful.

1. Talk about the 5W (namely who, when, what, where, why) information related to a topic. For example,
   · *Why are you studying English?*
   · I am studying English for work. Actually, I want to get a promotion soon. So, I study English Monday to Friday at a language institute. **(Why, When, Where)**

2. Follow an order to introduce your topic or make explanations. Expressions to list details or reasons include: First, Second, And third. For example,

Example 1

There are three key features of New York City. *First*, New York City is known for all of the places it has to shop. Many people come from all around the world just to shop there. *Second*, it is a melting pot of people from many different countries. This makes New York City a very interesting city to live in. *The third key feature of New York City is* the nightlife. No matter what time it is, you will always find something to do in New York City.

Example 2

There were several reasons why I would go to that library. *First*, it was right next to my dormitory building, so it only took me a few seconds to get there. *Second*, before a test, I would go to my favorite spot in the library to study. That spot was in a corner of the third floor and next to a large window where I had a bird's-eye view of the school campus. *And third*, I would go to the library to do research and find sources of information for my research papers.

Other expressions that you might want to use in organizing your thoughts include:

At first, afterwards, finally *(in time order)*
The first step, next, the last step *(process)*
Number 1 reason is ..., what's more important is ..., finally... *(importance or reason)*

The first thing I should mention is ...
The point I'd like to begin with is ...

Another point which I could add is that ...
A second feature which I should mention is that ...

And I shouldn't forget to mention that ...
In addition to what I've just said, I can add that ...
Something else that I need to comment on is that ...

The following items contain important vocabulary from the talk about "how to improve your sense of direction". Work with a partner and match vocabulary terms with their definitions. Consult a dictionary if necessary.

_____ 1. **Navigation** skills seem to come naturally to some—but others aren't so lucky.

_____ 2. First, a **confession**: I had a special interest in researching this topic because my own sense of direction is absolutely rubbish.

_____ 3. I'm determined to give my navigation skills a much-needed **boost**.

_____ 4. ... although the two approaches can be used **interchangeably**.

_____ 5. **Spatial** navigators see the bigger picture and always know where they are in relation to key landmarks ...

_____ 6. **Egocentric** navigators, meanwhile, tend to rely on detailed directions and local landmarks to break a journey into instalments...

_____ 7. By combining a few in one trip and **plotting** different routes to the same places, ...

_____ 8. This will come in particularly useful when you're doing the journey **in reverse**, ...

_____ 9. ... but this sudden burst of anxiety will only increase your **cognitive** load and ...

_____ 10. Ultimately, your sense of direction is a **use-it-or-lose-it** skill.

a. to draw a line by marking points on a graph

b. connected with the mental processes of understanding

c. the skill of planning a route

d. in a way that can be exchanged

e. If you don't use a skill often, you can't keep it.

f. in the opposite way

g. relating to space

h. a statement admitting something that you are ashamed or embarrassed about

i. centered in a person's own individual existence or perspective; thinking only of oneself

j. a strong push or big improvement

Task 2 *Listen to a talk about "how to improve your sense of direction" and choose the best answer.*

1. According to scientists, which are the two ways for people to navigate?

    A) vertical, horizontal

    B) physical, mental

    C) spatial, egocentric

    D) instinctive, sensible

2. Which of the following is correct about spatial navigators?

    A) They lose their way frequently.

    B) They are more intelligent.

    C) They never use maps.

    D) They see the bigger picture.

3. Which of the following is true about egocentric navigators?

    A) They rely on detailed directions and landmarks to split a journey and remember it.

    B) They will not fail in learning a route by heart if a road is closed.

    C) They know how to improve their sense of direction and keep working on it.

    D) They use only Satellite Navigation to work out where they had been.

4. What does the speaker suggest doing to improve one's sense of direction regarding the use of GPS?

    A) Update your GPS often.

    B) Don't rely on GPS too much.

    C) Buy a good GPS.

    D) Follow your GPS step by step.

5. What kind of skill is our sense of direction according to the speaker?

    A) instinctive skill

    B) physical skill

    C) technical skill

    D) skill of use-it-or-lose-it

Task 3   *Please paraphrase the following sentences by using your own words.*

> Finally, try to relax when you're on unfamiliar ground. It's all too easy to panic if you suspect you may be lost — but this sudden burst of anxiety will only increase your cognitive load and prevent you from calmly working out which way to go. Besides, getting lost is one of the best ways to discover new places and add more detail to that ever-growing mental map — both of which will help you become a better navigator in the long term.

Task 4   *Please discuss with your partners about the following questions. Try to use the speaking skills of organizing thoughts discussed in the previous part.*

1. What are the steps you will follow to find your way back when you get lost?

2. Do you agree that our sense of direction will deteriorate if using too much GPS? Why?

Criteria for Peer- / Self-Assessment

NO.	Analytic Items	Proportion	Peer- /Self-Assessment
1	Well-organized structure (5w information, related expressions to indicate organized thoughts (first, second, third, etc.)	20%	
2	Fluency (less accidental pauses, short pause length, less self-correction)	20%	
3	Accuracy (accuracy in using words and expressions, accuracy in grammar use)	20%	
4	Complexity (lexical variety, usage of less frequent vocabulary, syntactic complexity)	20%	
5	Pronunciation (no strong accent, correct stress, liaison, plosion in words and sentences, sounds naturally)	20%	
Total Score (use a 10-point scale)			

Part Five   Critical Thinking

Transport in China

Passage 1

Moving from Follower to Leader in Transport Technology

China's capacity for innovation in transport has strengthened — it possesses self-developed core technologies, and has made major breakthroughs in transport infrastructure and equipment. Capacity for sustainable development is growing. China is making steady progress from a follower to a leader in transport technology.

World-leading mega-projects

China leads the world in technology for railways at high altitudes and in extremely low temperatures, and for high-speed and heavy-haul（重型运输） railways. It has solved the most challenging technical problems confronting highway construction in difficult geological conditions such as plateau permafrost（高原冻土）, expansive soil, and desert. It also leads in core technologies for building deep-water offshore ports（近海港）, improving massive estuary（入海口）and long waterways, and building large airports.

Notable mega-projects include the Hong Kong — Zhuhai — Macao Bridge, the Xi'an — Chengdu High-speed Rail cutting through the Qinling Mountains, the automated container terminal at Qingdao Port, and the deep-water channel improvement project in the Yangtze River Estuary.

China leads the world in the total length and number of highway bridges and tunnels in service and under construction. It has seven of the ten longest cable-stayed bridges（斜拉桥）, six of the ten longest suspension bridges（吊桥）, six of the ten longest cross-sea bridges, and eight of the ten highest bridges in the world.

Accelerated development of intelligent transport

China is developing transport featuring Internet Plus to fully integrate modern information technology with transport management and services. The country has applied emerging technologies such as 5G, big data, and artificial intelligence to transport infrastructure and equipment, and has made breakthroughs in research and development of intelligent transport. Electronic ticketing and online booking have become increasingly popular in railway, highway, waterway and civil aviation passenger services, the application of IT in transport management has significantly increased. By the end of 2019, 229 airports and major airlines have realized paperless travel.

China has removed all expressway toll booths at provincial borders across the country. Positive results have been achieved in the application of new technologies such as Electronic Toll Collection (ETC) on expressways. By the end of 2019, there were more than 200 million ETC users across the country. Round-the-clock, all-weather and full-coverage monitoring of the road network and information distribution are strengthening.

Intelligent highway technologies are also promoted, and intelligent port and shipping technologies are widely used. Intelligent delivery outlets are found everywhere in all major cities, and automated sorting has been adopted by all major distribution centers of express delivery enterprises.

Development of transport in China is opening new fields for quality economic growth, injecting new vitality into economic and social development, and paving the way to a better life for the Chinese people.

Adapted from "Sustainable Development of Transport in China", Xinhuanet.com

Passage 2

Travel around East China's Shandong by Circular High-Speed Rail

A high-speed railway <u>linking</u> Rizhao <u>and</u> Qufu in east China's Shandong Province <u>started operation</u> on Tuesday. Not only is it the first high-speed railway for Linyi City in the south of the province, but <u>it also marks the formation of</u> China's second circular high-speed railway after the one in Hainan, south China.

Starting from Jinan West Railway Station, the high-speed rail line circles eight cities in Shandong, including Weifang, Qingdao, Linyi, Qufu and Tai'an in a six-hour train journey, offering visitors a more convenient and efficient way to explore Shandong. CGTN Travel is here to tell you what you mustn't miss along the railway line.

Jinan — the capital city of Shandong

It's said that Jinan is home to 72 springs scattered across the city, hence its nickname "City of Springs". Of its various attractions, Daming Lake, Baotu Spring and Thousand Buddha Mountain are the three best-known tourist destinations in Jinan.

Qingdao — a vibrant seaside city

You probably have heard of Qingdao beer. The beverage was born in the coastal city of Qingdao, but it's not the only attraction. Surrounded by the sea on three sides, the city lures numerous visitors with its enchanting seascape.

Linyi — an eco-friendly city

The landscape of Linyi is evenly divided into mountains, hills and flat land. This June, Yimeng Mountain has been listed as a Global Geopark by UNESCO for its rich natural resources. At the foot of the mountain, there is a blanket of lush green trees and vegetation. If you reach the top of the peak, you be rewarded with endless and mesmerizing views.

Qufu — the home town of China's great philosopher

Qufu has numerous historic palaces, temples and cemeteries, and is best known as the home town of Confucius (551–479 BC) — a great philosopher in Chinese history. The three most famous cultural sites of the city are all related to him, respectively the Confucius Temple, Confucius Cemetery and the Kong Family Mansion.

Tai'an — a city centered on Mount Tai

Widely regarded as the best of the "Five Great Mountains of China," Mount Tai features striking cliffs, deep canyons and incredible peaks. The tallest peak is the Jade Emperor Peak, soaring over 1,500 meters in height. Nowadays, visitors often stop by temples to pray as they climb the mountain — just as the deceased emperors once did — asking for health and good fortune for themselves and their families.

Train tickets can be purchased at railway stations or via the official online ticketing website. The ticket price for a second-class seat is 384 yuan and 619 yuan for first class.

Adapted from the article by CGTN

Task 1 *Read Passage 1 and discuss the following questions.*

How do you feel about the changes of China's transport in the past few years? In what way do you think it affects our daily life? Write down some key words below (based on the passage or your own opinion) for your detailed answer before you get ready to speak.

	Information from the Passage	Your Own Opinion
Point 1		
Point 2		
Point 3		

Task 2 *Read Passage 2 and underline the collocations. The first paragraph has been done for you. Pay attention to the expressions that describe the features of the cities in Shandong. Write them down below.*

City	Collocations & Descriptive Words
Jinan	
Qingdao	
Linyi	
Qufu	
Tai'an	

Task 3 *Have a discussion with your partners about the following questions based on your reading.*

1. Which public transport do you use most often in China and how do you feel about it?
2. Which city in Shandong do you probably want to visit in future and why?

Task 4 *Listen to a lecture entitled "5 Reasons Why Cycling to Work Will Improve Your Life" and fill in the blanks according to what you hear.*

1. _____ to get on to an _____ train only to stand with your face up against a tall man's back is yet to be acknowledged as _____ of

good mental health.

2. Cycling to work, on the other hand will boost your energy levels, make you more alert, aid _____ — as well as giving you _____.

3. _____ could burn hundreds, if not thousands of calories a week, with little impact on your joints. Of course, the benefits of regular exercise go far beyond how much you weigh: _____ of regular activity will also _____ and reduce risk of _____.

4. When you cycle to work, you _____ to your town or city — and discover the life that lies between and around train stations and crowded commuter streets.

5. You'll also be _____. Just imagine if every cyclist you saw on your daily commute was instead in a car, on a bus, on a train – things would be a lot more _____.

6. So not only are you making your own life more _____, _____, you're also easing the grind (乏味的工作) up for everyone else too.

Task 5 *Listen to the lecture again and choose the best answer according to what you have heard.*

1. What is the article about?

   A) The benefits of cycling to work.

   B) The drawbacks of cycling to work.

   C) The physical risks of cycling to work.

   D) The huge expenses of cycling to work.

2. Which of the following is true about cycling to work?

   A) It can increase your stress.

   B) It can cause health problems.

   C) It can boost economic market.

   D) It can boost your energy level.

3. Why is cycling to work good for your health?

   A) It can increase the risk of chronic illness.

   B) It can relieve your pain of illness.

   C) It can burn calories and help people get fit.

   D) It can increase your pleasure of life.

4. What is another advantage of cycling to work?

   A) It is a good chance to stay away from public transport.

B) It is a good chance to explore your city.

C) It saves you time.

D) It saves your energy.

5. What is an additional benefit of cycling to work?

A) It could reduce CO_2 emission and congestion.

B) It could eliminate CO_2 and air pollution

C) It could increase bike sales and circulation.

D) It could strengthen your cycling skills.

Task 6   *Please compare people's attitudes toward travelling between now and in the past in China. What are the differences?*

NO.	Travelling Now	Travelling in the Past
1		
2		
3		

Task 7   *Please share your idea with your partner about one of the following statements.*

1. Travelling is the best way to learn about other cultures.

2. Travelling on a budget can be as enjoyable.

3. The world is a book, and those who do not travel read only a page.

4. The traveler sees what he sees. The tourist sees what he has come to see.

5. When preparing to travel, lay out all your clothes and all your money. Then take half the clothes and twice the money.

6. The most important trip you may take in life is meeting people halfway.

Part Six Encountering IELTS Speaking

Words and Expressions about Travelling & Transportation

big/ huge city 大城市

international city 国际都市

24-hour city 不夜城

metropolis 大都会

autonomous region 自治区

small town 小城市 / 小镇

small village 村庄

special economic zone 经济特区

tourist city/attraction 旅游城市 / 景点

industrial city 工业城市

coastal city 海边城市

capital city 省会，首都

vibrant/vigorous city 有活力的城市

booming/prosperous city 欣欣向荣的城市

a city with long history 历史悠久的城市

appearance of a city 市容

be home to ... 以……出名

natural attraction 自然景点

spectacular/breathtaking scenery 壮丽的景色

high-rise building 高层建筑

skyscraper 摩天大楼

amusement park 游乐园

theme park 主题公园

botanical garden 植物园

blooming flowers 盛开的花

environmentally-friendly 对环境友好的

over-crowded 过度拥挤的

tourist season 旅游旺季

go sightseeing 观光

go camping 露营

go backpacking 背包旅行

go on holiday 度假

itinerary 行程

limited budget 有限的预算

destination 目的地

buy souvenir 买纪念品

landmark 地标

youth hostel 青年旅社

holiday inn 假日酒店

motel 汽车旅馆

check in/ out 入住登记 / 结账离开

interior 内部

exterior 外部

well-designed 设计得很好的

in good condition 状况良好

the hustle and bustle of a city 喧嚣

admission fee 门票

exhibition 展览

display 陈列

infrastructure 基础设施

rush hour 交通高峰期

traffic jam/congestion 交通堵塞

heavy traffic 交通繁忙

carpool 拼车

traffic rules 交通规则

traffic light 交通信号灯

speed limit 限速

speeding 超速

ticket 罚单

public transport 公共交通

parking lot 停车场

vehicle 交通工具

ferry 轮渡

cruise 游轮旅行

helicopter 直升机

airplane 飞机

airline 航空公司；航线

flight 航班

terminal 航站楼

customs 海关

take off/land 起飞 / 降落

delayed （航班）延误

boarding pass 登机牌

flight attendant 空乘人员

hand luggage/carry-on 随身行李

overweight luggage fee 超重行李费

security check 安检

metal detector 金属探测仪

X-ray scanner X 光扫描仪

flammable materials 易燃物品

aisle/window seat 靠走道 / 窗的座位

subway/metro 地铁

priority seat 爱心座位

commuter train 通勤火车

high-speed train 高铁

light rail 轻轨

train timetable 列车时刻表

arrival/departure time 到达 / 离开的时刻

platform 站台

automobile 汽车

cab/taxi 出租车

rental car 供出租的汽车

delivery truck 送货 / 快递货车

four-wheel drive 四驱车

sports car 跑车

sedan 轿车

pickup 皮卡（车）

school bus 校车

ambulance 救护车

fire engine 消防车

police car 警车

dump truck 垃圾车

forklift 叉车

crane 起重机，吊车

cement mixer 水泥搅拌车

van 面包车

shuttle （bus） 接驳车

electric car 电动汽车

fishing boat 渔船

lifeboat 救生艇

mountain bike 山地自行车

scooter 滑板车

trailer 拖车，活动的房车

passenger 乘客

pedestrian 行人

commuter 通勤者；（远距离）上下班
往返的人

delivery man 快递员

gas station 加油站

one-way ticket 单程票

round-trip ticket 双程票

monthly/season ticket 月票

cycle lane 自行车道

bus lane 公交车道

overpass 过街天桥

bypass/ring road 环线

highway/free way/express way 高速公路

IELTS Speaking Criterion — Grammatical Range and Accuracy

In IELTS Speaking Test, a key component is demonstrating a range of grammar (see Table 5–1 for reference). The range of grammar includes using a variety of complex structures. These are sentences with multiple bits of information, as opposed to single bits of information. For example,

> Just beside the station was a stadium, which was built in the 19th century, and where games are now held every weekend.

Students are not expected to be 100% accurate in speaking, but control in grammar usage is important. Also, don't be afraid to correct your mistakes when you are speaking if you realize you have made any.

Suggestions for improvement in grammar

1. Record yourself and listen back afterwards.
2. Be aware of the grammatical mistakes in your speeches.
3. Practice reconstructing sentences.
4. Practice linking words and expressions.
5. Pay attention to past tense of common verbs for Part 2 questions of IELTS Speaking Test.

Table 5–1   IELTS Speaking Test Band Descriptors of Grammar

Band	Descriptors of Grammar
9	■ uses a full range of structures naturally and appropriately ■ produces consistently accurate structures apart from 'slips' characteristic of native speaker speech
8	■ uses a wide range of structures flexibly ■ produces a majority of error-free sentences with only very occasional inappropriacies or basic/non-systematic errors
7	■ uses a range of complex structures with some flexibility ■ frequently produces error-free sentences though some grammatical mistakes persist
6	■ uses a mix of simple and complex structures, but with limited flexibility ■ may make frequent mistakes with complex structures though these rarely cause comprehension problems
5	■ produces basic sentence forms with reasonable accuracy ■ uses a limited range of more complex structures, but these usually contain errors and may cause some comprehension problems

Task 1 *Please rewrite the sentences below following the example. Use 5W (who, what, when, where, why) information to make it more complex.*

Example

[Original] I like ice cream.

[Improved] I like to eat ice cream <u>after work at Diary Queen because I love cold desserts</u>.
        (*when, where, why*)

1. The man was explaining how to use the computer.

   _____

2. They are having a discussion.

   _____

Task 2 *Talk about "What areas need to be improved for Chinese tourism?" for one minute and record yourself. Have your partner listen to your recording and see if there can be any improvement in terms of grammatical range and accuracy. You can jot down the key points in the following box.*

```



```

IELTS Speaking Test Items

Part 1

1. Do you like your home town? Why?

2. Is your home town suitable for young people to live in?

3. Is there anything you would like to change in your home town?

4. What interesting things can we do in big cities?

5. Do you prefer to be a driver or a passenger?

6. Where have you travelled?

7. What kind of places do you like to travel to?

8. Would you rather travel alone or with friends and family?

9. What do you dislike about travelling?

10. How do you prepare for a trip?

11. What do you think causes the serious traffic problems?

12. What are the advantages of riding bicycles?

▶ **Sample Answer**

2. Is your home town suitable for young people to live in?

Definitely yes, the city of Xi'an is a perfect place for young people to live in simply because it has lots of things for young generation to enjoy themselves, such as good sports facilities, convenient public transport, excellent restaurants, beautiful parks, and various interesting leisure activities.

4. What interesting things can we do in big cities?

We can have a lot of fun in big cities. If you like shopping, you could go shopping for beautiful clothes and see the designs of famous brands. We have to admit that major museums are usually located in big cities. In these places, we can appreciate our culture and history. There're also some amusement parks and leisure centers for people both young and old.

5. Do you prefer to be a driver or a passenger?

Generally speaking, I would rather be a passenger mainly because it makes me less stressful and nervous. I don't need to pay my attention to the traffic, and I can spend time doing something like reading books or listening to music on my phone.

Part 2

1. Describe a trip you had.

You should say:

Who you traveled with;

Where you went;

What you did or saw;

And explain why you want to talk about this trip.

2. Describe a place you would go to visit in the future.

You should say:

Where it is;

How would you go there;

Who would you go with;

And explain why you would like to go to this place about this trip.

3. Describe a building in a school or university that you attended.

You should say:

Where it is;

What it looks like;

What it is used for;

And explain what facilities it has.

4. Describe a historic place that you enjoyed visiting.

You should say:

Where it was;

When you went there;

What it was like;

And explain why you liked it.

5. Describe the ideal home (flat or house) that you would like to live in.

You should say:

Where it would be;

What type of house it would be;

How you would decorate it (or, how you would furnish it);

And explain why you would like to live in this kind of home.

▶ **Sample Answer**

Most people have the experience of dreaming about their ideal house. I also have my ideal house in mind.

The location should be in the suburbs, because I can have more space to build a big house and to plant my own garden. Our family is a big family, so the house will have 3 stories and a basement. I'll place a piano on the first floor because our family members all like classical music. All the bedrooms will be arranged on the second floor. Each room should have its unique design. My parents are traditional people, so their bedroom should be decorated in traditional Chinese style. I like western style decorations, so different kinds of oil paintings in my room will be indispensable.

The 3rd floor is the most special floor, because my father and I are movie lovers and watching films is our biggest hobby. I will place a home cinema projector there, so we could enjoy good films at home. The basement will serve as a storage room for our family, so the house would always look neat.

This is my ideal house, but I need money to fulfill my dream. I'll try my best to make enough money for this house and I hope I don't need to wait for too long.

Part 3

1. What are the differences of transportation means now and in the past?
2. What are the advantages and disadvantages of owing a car?
3. What do you think causes the serious traffic problems?
4. What should governments do to solve traffic problems?
5. How can a place attract more tourists to visit?
6. Will tourists affect the local people's life?
7. Will you travel abroad through travel agencies or will you travel abroad on yourself?
8. What kind of problems will you encounter on a trip?
9. What are the benefits of travelling abroad?
10. What do you think the public transportations in the future would be like?
11. What are the things you don't love about transport in your country?
12. Do you agree that travelers can be the burden of the environment in the local places?
13. Do you think that travelling alone is more exciting than travelling in groups?

▶ **Sample Answer**

1. What are the differences of transportation means now and in the past?

   Well, there are many differences in ways of transportation now and in the past. For example, people now can travel around by bus, by plane, by car, by bicycle, and by underground railway. However, these may not be possible in the past, when people could only choose to travel on foot, on horses or by boats. Therefore, people now are enabled to travel faster, safer and farther.

2. What are the advantages and disadvantages of owing a car?

It can be a great convenience to own a car. One of the main advantages of owning a car is that it is convenient for long distance travel. It's easier for you to carry as much luggage as you want with you in a car. Another good thing about owning a car is weather protection. You can always sit in a car comfortably while it is bitter cold weather outside the car. One more great thing about car ownership is that it saves a lot of time compared to public transportation.

However, having a car can be inconvenient too. For example, in many cities, owing a car could cause you to get stuck in the traffic jam because cars are not as moveable as bicycles or motorbikes. Moreover, finding parking space can be a problem because there are not a lot of areas for car parking in major cities, let alone the high parking fees in big cities. Although sometimes good cars show people how rich you are, they do cost a lot of money whether it is to buy one or to keep one.

4. What should governments do to solve traffic problems?

First of all, I really think that the government should encourage people to use public transport as much as possible, instead of driving private cars to address traffic problems. I think it would be a good idea to actually reveal the total amount of emissions released by a car during a thirty-minute drive, and to compare it to other scary quantities of carbon monoxide produced by different vehicles. The aim would be to make people realize that pollution is a serious matter. In my home town, the government has decided to widen the roads, but actually, this decision simply encourages more people to buy their own vehicles. I really think that buses should have their own lanes on the road. Buses would run faster and traffic would be more efficient from one bus stop to another. Finally, everyone needs to realize that driving a car can be dangerous. In China, since driving is fairly new (quite new) to people, people only see the fun of it. They only think that driving offers a great feeling of freedom and comfort, but they should also be conscious that thousands of people die on the roads every year.

8. What kind of problems will you encounter on a trip?

When we are travelling to somewhere else, especially the places that are far away from our home town, or the places that we are unfamiliar with, we may encounter various problems. For example, we may be unaccustomed to the weather or the foods there, or we may get hurt and do not know how to get treated. In some other cases, we may get stuck in misunderstandings with the local people. Therefore, we have to be well-prepared when we want to have a trip.

9. What are the benefits of travelling abroad?

Travelling abroad may help us to broaden our sight by enabling us to view different scenery, meet different people, taste different foods, and experience different cultures. In addition, by travelling abroad, we may feel far away from the life at home, and so better relax ourselves. Besides, having a fresher eye about the world and learning something new or more advanced from the country we visit may also be possible.

Checklist for This Chapter

Please check according to the scale from 1 to 5.

(1 — Strongly Disagree; 2 — Disagree; 3 — Undecided; 4 —Agree; 5 — Strongly Agree)

Can-do List	1	2	3	4	5
I am familiar with travel- or transport-related questions & expressions.					
I can use classification expressions to organize ideas.					
I know how to describe places, how to talk about travelling and transportation.					
I am more aware of using complex and correct sentences in speaking.					

Self-reflection

1. In which part have I done very well?

2. In which part should I make improvement?

3. What should I do to bridge the current gap?

4. What suggestions do I have for my teacher or the class arrangement?

5. Anything I would like to say.

(Your reflection could be written in Chinese)

6

Family and Children

LEARNING OBJECTIVES

In this chapter you will learn

- how to describe an object
- how to compare and contrast two things/items
- how to develop answers by using deductive pattern
- the significance of scientific educational notion

Part One   Warming-up

Task 1   *Talk to a partner about one of your family members for 20 seconds each. You may jot down the key words in the following box while preparing for your description.*

1. father

2. mother

3. brother

4. sister

5. grandmother
6. grandfather

Task 2　*Please list the things you miss most when you are away from home. You may discuss with your partners and compare your discussion results with other groups.*

NO.	Things You Miss Most When You Are Away from Home
1	
2	
3	
4	

Task 3　*Listen to people talking about what they miss most when they are away from home. Then fill the blanks in the following sentences.*

1. Erm ... one thing I miss, living in England, is the food from back home, all the _____ and the _____ of going to the farmers market to buy fresh cottage cheese from a lady that your grandma has known since you were little.

2. That's right. _____, _____, tomatoes just don't _____ in this country!

3. Yeah, and it seems that the most _____ here is a ripe watermelon. I keep buying them, but every single one is a _____, I'll always miss the watermelons we used to get from the south of Ukraine.

4. Hmm, that's right. So, ... erm, enough about food. What I miss most is the language. There is _____ walking along the street and _____ you are part of something bigger than yourself... hearing your own language. I always feel a bit ... erm ... small when I'm abroad and all I hear is a foreign language. It's like Fm a bit _____ and I'm ... I'm missing something. It's hard to explain.

5. Mmm, I know _____. Also, I find it hard to be away from home on national holidays. Some of our traditions are just impossible to _____. Er, you just don't get the same feeling of people coming together to celebrate in the streets.

Adapted from New Headway, 4th edition

Part Two   IELTS Speaking Test

Talking about an Object

To give a good monologue about an object in IELTS Speaking Test Part 2, you can refer to the following order of description.
1) What it is and why you have it.
2) What it looks like.
3) What its purpose/function is.
4) Evaluate it.
5) Why it is important and how you feel about it.

Here are some words and expressions you can use in describing an object.
1) What does it look like

material	plastic, wood, metal, silver, copper, wool, cotton, marble
color	brown, purple, light blue, dark grey, pure green, sky blue
shape	heart-shaped, round, oval, curved, rectangular, square, spherical, triangular
size	compact, tiny, huge / enormous, life-sized

2) Function
■ The electronic dictionary serves as a **practical study tool**.

- The vase is mainly used **for decoration**.
- I often use my bike to **take a road trip** with my buddies.
- The major function of my iPad is to **contact my family**.
- This bag will **come in handy** when I go travelling because I can put a lot of stuff in it.

3) Why important
- This photo often **reminds me of** my childhood, which is the happiest time of my life.
- My phone has **enriched my world** because I can always have fun with it.
- My bike brings a lot of **convenience** to my daily life and I can keep fit at the same time.
- The trophy **symbolizes my hard work.** Whenever I see it, I will tell myself nothing is impossible if I put my heart into it.

Task 1 *Please read the following passage and notice the function of each paragraph.*

Topic: Describe a toy you liked in your childhood.

Say what it is and why you have it.

As early as four years old, I already enjoyed swimming since my family's residence was close to a slow-moving and tranquil lake in the country. I spent most of my weekends playing with my mom and dad at the lake. **When my uncle learned that I was more than eager to swim in the lake, he bought me an inflatable swim ring with a rubber yellow duck squeaker toy as a freebie.**

Say what its purpose is.

It's still vivid in my memory how elated I was when I got those presents from my uncle during his once-a-year visit to our tiny house. I didn't really pay much attention to the swim ring but I was so focused on the rubber yellow duck squeaker toy that he gave me. **I was entertained playing it and that made me burst into laughter every time I squeezed it for innumerable times.** The sound it created was strange to me and at the same time, really hilarious. I might not realize it then, how noisy it was for my parents and my uncle.

Evaluate it.

Anyway, whenever I played with my parents at the lake, I always had my squeaker with me. I built a castle with my squeaker at the shore, swam with it and pretended to be a lifesaver when it moved far away from me. **I could say, I really had a wonderful and memorable time with that favorite toy of mine. It was like my buddy whenever I spent time at the lake.**

As I was the only child, I created a special kind of bond with my toys, most especially with that yellow duck squeaker. Interestingly, every time I see some squeakers these days,

I always have a bittersweet feeling — realizing how beautiful the innocence I had when I was still a child and learning how time flies.

Say why it is important and how you feel about it.

Task 2 *Please share your idea with your partners about the following topics. You may refer to the above order of description.*

1. Describe a toy you liked most in your childhood.
2. Describe your favorite food when you were young.

Part Three   Speaking after Reading

Parents' Stress and Depression "Rise during Lockdowns"

Levels of stress, depression and anxiety among parents and carers have increased with the pressures of the lockdowns, suggests research from the University of Oxford. Issues include difficulty relaxing, feeling hopeless and being irritable. Many parents, especially those of secondary-age pupils, say they are worried about their children's futures. The government has said it is aware how challenging it is for parents to support children with home learning. The **research**, based on responses from 6,246 parents and carers between mid-March and the end of December 2020, found problems including:

- difficulty relaxing
- being easily upset or agitated
- feeling hopeless
- lacking interest and pleasure
- feeling fearful and worried
- being more irritable, over-reactive and impatient

On an established scale of depression, anxiety and stress, parents' depression scores increased from April through to June from an average of 9.03 to 9.71, says the study funded by the Economic and Social Research Council. While these average scores decreased over the summer, to a low of 8.23 in September, they rose again over the course of the autumn term to a high of 10.1 points in December.

Parents' stress scores were at their lowest in August and September at 11.4 points, but increased to a high of 13.2 in December, following the pre-Christmas lockdown. The researchers said higher levels of stress were detected particularly in low-income families, as well as single-parent households and those with children with special educational needs.

While average anxiety scores were relatively stable throughout the whole period — ranging from a 4.71 points in April to 4.24 in July — they hit a high of 5 points in December. The study also found just over a third (36%) of parents with young children (10 years or younger) said they were "substantially worried" about their children's behaviour, in contrast to just over a quarter (28%) of parents who had older children only (11 years or older). However, nearly half (45%) of those with secondary-age children were worried about their children's education and future, compared to 32% of those with young children.

Leticea, a parent who took part in the study, said: "I think that UK leaders should have access to this data to see what is going on with the mental health of families and how they are being affected by COVID-19 with increased levels of stress, depression and anxiety — we need something to look forward to." I am also worried that the next three months will show a sharper increase in anxiety and stress where parents are having to do more teaching at home. "Children are more worried as their teachers are becoming ill — the 'new variant' sounds more scary, my daughter keeps commenting on an increasing worry of getting ill which she didn't do so much before." Another parent, Madiha, said: "Current times are hard enough as they are. " As a working parent, the most important thing for me is to ensure my family's wellbeing, their safety, and their continued development. "Prolonged screen time, disruption to daily routine, frequent arguments, lack of exercise, and stress of exams have all been contributing factors to our mental health and wellbeing." Madiha said she hoped the study would play a part in informing policy and developing interventions to help families.

Cathy Creswell, professor of clinical developmental psychology at Oxford University and co-leader of the study, said the findings showed parents were particularly vulnerable to distress during the first lockdown. "Our data highlight the particular strains felt by parents during lockdown when many feel that they have been spread too thin by the demands of meeting their children's needs during the pandemic, along with home-schooling and work commitments." John Jolly, head of the charity Parentkind, said the research highlighted "the additional stress and pressure that partial school closures place on parents". Given the disruption to family life, it is vital that policymakers consult and listen to the concerns of parents on issues that directly impact them and their children's futures. "This includes the safety and reopening of schools, the fair allocation of grades in the absence of exams, and remote learning provision." The Oxford researchers are tracking children's and parents' mental health throughout the current crisis, to help them identify what protects young people from deteriorating mental health and how this may vary according to child and family characteristics.

Adapted from https://www.bbc.co.uk/news/education-55707322

Word Bank

agitate	*v.* to make someone feel worried or angry 激怒；使不安；使烦乱
fund	*n.* an amount of money saved, collected, or provided for a particular purpose 基金；专款
restriction	*n.* an official limit on something 限制规定；限制法规
detect	*v.* to notice something that is partly hidden or not clear, or to discover something, especially using a special method 发现；查明；侦察出
substantially	*adv.* to a large degree 非常；大大地
variant	*n.* something that is slightly different from other similar things 变种；变体；变形
scary	*adj.* making you feel frightened 恐怖的；吓人的
prolong	*v.* to make something last a longer time 延长
intervention	*n.* the action of becoming intentionally involved in a difficult situation, in order to improve it or prevent it from getting worse 出面；介入
vulnerable	*adj.* able to be easily physically, emotionally, or mentally hurt, influenced, or attacked 脆弱的，易受伤害的
strain	*n.* a force or influence that stretches, pulls, or puts pressure on something, sometimes causing damage 压力；重负
pandemic	*n.* (of a disease) existing in almost all of an area or in almost all of a group of people, animals, or plants 流行病；大流行病
allocation	*n.* the process of giving someone their part of a total amount of something to use in a particular way 划拨的款项；拨给的场地；分配的东西
provision	*n.* the act of providing something 提供；供给；准备
deteriorate	*v.* to become worse 恶化，变坏

https://dictionary.cambridge.org/

Read the article and pick up the best choice.

1. Which of the following condition will NOT cause people to become more stressful?

   A) Low-income families.

   B) Parents who had older children only (11 years or older).

   C) Parents with children with special educational needs.

   D) Single-parent families.

2. What is the attitude of Leticea towards the study funded by the Economic and Social Research Council?

   A) Suspicious.

   B) Objective.

   C) Disappointed.

   D) Favorable.

3. Which of the questions is answered in the last paragraph?

   A) Why should we pay more attention to parents' distress in their life?

   B) Why is it important that policymakers consult and listen to the concerns of parents?

   C) Why are parents particularly vulnerable to strains during the lockdown?

   D) What actions should parents do to protect their children from mental health problems?

4. What is the best title for the 3rd paragraph?

   A) Fearful and Worried

   B) Frequent Arguments

   C) Particularly Vulnerable

   D) Children's Wellbeing

Task 2   *Please share ideas with your partners about the following questions based on what you read.*

1. How does the pandemic affect people's daily life?

2. Why were parents with young children (10 years or younger) at higher level of stress than those who had older children only (11 years or older)?

3. What should the government do to mitigate the effects of pandemic?

Task 3   *Please retell the following short paragraph by using your own words.*

Levels of stress, depression and anxiety among parents and carers have increased with the pressures of the lockdowns, suggests research from the University of Oxford. Issues include difficulty relaxing, feeling hopeless and being irritable. Many parents, especially those of secondary-age pupils, say they are worried about their children's futures. The government has said it is aware how challenging it is for parents to support children with home learning.

Task 4 *Please make a survey among your peers and report the result of your survey in class. You are recommended to do the survey with your group members. The following questions may be included in your survey.*

1. Why do/don't they want to study at home?
2. What are the pros and cons of home teaching?
3. What did the Chinese government do about teaching and learning during the COVID-19 pandemic?
4. Do they prefer online courses or face-to-face courses in classroom?
5. What are the consequences of COVID-19 pandemic on education?

Part Four   Speaking after Listening

IELTS Speaking Skill — Comparing and Contrast

Comparing and contrasting are ways of exploring the similarities and differences between two things. Generally speaking, comparing is showing the similarities, and contrasting is showing differences between two things that are related in some way. For example, you wouldn't compare/contrast reading a book to driving a car, but you would compare reading a book to reading with an e-reader.

The following are some words and expressions you can use in comparing or contrasting two things.

Types: The signal words of comparison

Definition

■ The words that indicate similarity in meaning, such as "like", "alike", "similar to" and so on.
■ The words that express parallel in structure, such as "either ... or ... ", "not only ... but also ... ", "both ... and ... " and so on.

Sentence structure

There are several similarities between A and B.

A and B have the same view of ...

A and B have a lot in common.

In common with A, B prefers ...

A resembles B in that A is also interested in ...

Just as A likes to ..., B likes to ....

Like A, B likes ....

A likes .... The same with A, B also likes ...

A and B are the same in that they both ...

A and B have the same ...

A likes ...; similarly, B likes ...

Both A and B have ...

Types: The signal words of contrast

Definition

- The words that express "difference" in meaning, such as "be different from", "differ from" and so on.

- The words that present comparative degree, such as "faster ... than", "taller ... than" and so on.

- The words that indicate a turning or concession, such as "though", "but" and so on.

Sentence structure

Unlike A, B likes outdoor sports.

In contrast to A, B likes outdoor sports.

Different from A, B likes outdoor sports.

Contrary to A, B likes outdoor sports.

As opposed to A, B ...

A is different from B in that B ...

A differs from B in that B ...

A contrasts with B in that B ...

A likes ...; however / in contrast / by contrast/ on the other hand, B likes ...

A likes...; B, however, likes ...

A likes..., but B likes ...

A likes ..., whereas / while B likes ...

A is not as ... as B.

A is more / less ... than B.

Task 1   *The following items contain important vocabulary from the lecture — How to raise successful kids without over parenting. Work with a partner and match vocabulary terms with their definitions. Check your answers in a dictionary if necessary.*

_____ 1. It's just that there's a certain style of parenting these days that is kind of messing up kids, **impeding** their chances to develop into themselves ...

_____ 2. ... where parents feel a kid can't be successful unless the parent is protecting and preventing at every turn and **hovering** over every happening ...

_____ 3. ... and micromanaging every moment, and **steering** their kid towards some small subset of colleges and careers ...

_____ 4. ... we spend so much time nudging, hinting, helping, haggling, nagging as the case may be, to be sure they're not **screwing up**, not closing doors, not ruining their future ...

_____ 5. And our kids, regardless of where they end up at the end of high school, they're breathless. They're **brittle**.

_____ 6. And they're **withering** now under high rates of anxiety and depression and some of them are wondering, will this life ever turn out to have been worth it?

_____ 7. Or maybe, maybe, we're just afraid they won't have a future we can **brag** about to our friends and with stickers on the backs of our cars.

_____ 8. That is not what I'm saying. What I'm saying is, when we treat grades and scores and **accolades** and awards as the purpose of childhood ...

_____ 9. ... I think I was treating my Sawyer and Avery like little bonsai trees — that I was going to carefully clip and **prune** and shape into some perfect form of a human that might just be perfect enough to warrant them admission to one of the most highly selective colleges.

_____ 10. ... and it's my job to provide a nourishing environment, to strengthen them through **chores** and to love them so they can love others and receive love and the college ...

a. to stay in the air in one place

b. to take control of a situation and influence the way in which it develops

c. hard but easily broken

d. to delay or stop the progress of sth

e. a task that you do regularly / an unpleasant or boring task

f. cause something to fail or be spoiled

g. to cut off some of the branches from a tree, bush, etc. so that it will grow better and stronger

h. to talk too proudly about sth you own or sth you have done

i. praise or an award for an achievement that people admire

j. to become less or weaker, especially before disappearing completely

Task 2 *Listen to a talk about "parenting", and pick up the best choice.*

1. Which style of parenting is mentioned in the talk?

A) A type of parenting that will help children develop into themselves.

B) A type of parenting that parents are very interested in.

C) A type of parenting that will prevent children from growing up freely.

D) A type of parenting that many parenting experts use.

2. According to the talk, what is parents' belief of their children's success?

A) To finish high school successfully.

B) To get into some specific colleges or careers.

C) Free of anxiety and depression.

D) To have a future they can brag to their friends.

3. Why does the professor mention "What was great about lunch today?"

A) To encourage parents to take an interest in their children's life.

B) To emphasize that lunch is quite important for children.

C) To encourage parents to learn the definition of success.

D) To emphasize that parents should spend more time with their kids.

4. How many children does the professor have?

A) Five.   B) Four.

C) Three.   D) Two.

5. According to the professor, which of the following is NOT a good way to treat your kids?

A) To support them in becoming their glorious selves.

B) To strengthen them through chores.

C) To love them so they can love others and receive love.

D) To carefully clip and prune and shape into some perfect form of a human.

Task 3 *Please paraphrase the following sentence by using your own words.*

Well, we parents, we parents are pretty sure it's all worth it. We seem to behave — it's like we literally think they will have no future if they don't get into one of these tiny set of colleges or careers we have in mind for them. Or maybe,

maybe, we're just afraid they won't have a future we can brag about to our friends and with stickers on the backs of our cars.

Task 4 *Please discuss with your partners about the following questions. Try to use the speaking skills of comparing and contrasting discussed in the previous part.*

1. What are the differences between educational notion among Chinese parents in the past and now?
2. Can you compare the education notion of your parents and that you think ideal?
3. What are the differences between children nowadays and children in the past?
4. Can you compare your childhood and that of your parents?

Criteria for Peer- / Self-Assessment

NO.	Analytic Items	Proportion	Peer- /Self-Assessment
1	Using expressions of comparison or contrast properly	20%	
2	Fluency (less accidental pauses, short pause length, less self-correction)	20%	
3	Accuracy (accuracy in using words and expressions, accuracy in grammar use)	20%	
4	Complexity(lexical variety, usage of less frequent vocabulary, syntactic complexity)	20%	
5	Pronunciation (no strong accent, correct stress, liaison, plosion in words and sentences)	20%	
Total Score (use a 10-point scale)			

Driving Kids to School

In the 1970s and 1980s most of us walked or rode a bike to primary school without thinking too much about it. Cars were expensive and few families had more than one, so if your school was close and the rain or heat wasn't terrible, walking or cycling was the most obvious way to get there. My family has been very lucky to live close to a local school situated near good public transport, and walking to school has always been part of our routine. When my two boys were too young to walk or cycle on their own, it was easy to walk with them as part of my journey to work. Leaving the house for school in those days felt like escaping through a magical sliding door — from the rush and stress of the school morning routine to a slower, calmer world. Once outside the door, irritation about lost lunchboxes and last-minute permission slips would dissipate. Our paces matched. I got to hear a bit more about what was going on in their young lives and minds. Then there is the quiet pleasure of the walk itself: the unscheduled but happy meeting of a favorite friend or animal along the way, the seasonal scoffing of mulberries overhanging a laneway en route, the complicit exchanges of harried parents, a sudden waft of jasmine announcing spring. Walking to school helps us to feel as though we're living in a real neighborhood and community that only footfall on pathways can create. The benefits of living as much as possible outside of the urgent, car-driven world seem obvious.

Fewer kids walk or bike to school

Today we drive our kids to school in record numbers. The national rate of "active travel to school", as the experts call it, has declined over the past 40 years from 75 to 25 per cent of trips. Much of this can be explained by growing car ownership, changing family dynamics and increasing distances between some homes and schools. But there have also been changes in how far kids are allowed or are willing to go. Nearly 60 per cent of Australian parents report that the distance from home to school is three kilometers or less. It's a trend that's reflected in many other OECD countries and worries policymakers in the fields of both health and transport. Health professionals estimate that more than 70 per cent of children and 91 per cent of young people do not meet minimum physical activity recommendations. But it's also a transport issue. In recent years I have worked with other transport policymakers and planners on how future transport systems can keep up with growing populations. The research clearly shows small changes in people's travel behavior to make fewer car trips can make a big difference in how the transport system copes.

Parents are role models

Whether we like it or not, parents are role models and habits are formative. "Active travel to school" is one of 10 priority areas proposed by the Australian Health Policy Collaboration and more than 70 leading chronic disease experts to fix the growing obesity and chronic health crisis. And you don't have to be a transport professional to see that school trips in cars are also bad for traffic congestion and road safety. Queues of cars around schools and local roundabouts make crossings dangerous for walkers and cyclists. While these trips may seem short and innocuous, the sheer volume of them also clogs up the wider network, diminishing air quality and the way our cities function. Experts estimate that the additional congestion costs generated by school trips in cars is in the hundreds of millions of dollars. So what can we do to get more kids walking or riding a bike to school? Good pedestrian infrastructure, pleasant walking and cycling environments and safe crossings are critical, of course. The good news is that transport planners are increasingly seeing streets as places for walking or riding bikes, and pedestrians and cyclists as more than just safety risks to be mitigated. But parents' perceptions are also a key obstacle to more kids cycling and walking to school, particularly when the decision is to let them do this independently.

Could you be breaking the law?

It's not helpful that in some places letting a child go to school on their own could be classed as breaking the law. In 2017 the ABC reported on a notice published in a school newsletter bearing the Queensland Police Service insignia telling parents that children under the age of 12 cannot walk or ride to school alone. For the past 10 years, Queensland's criminal codes have made it an offence to leave a child under 12 unsupervised for an "unreasonable" time (although legally speaking the report argued that this was unlikely to mean a blanket ban on kids under 12 making their way to school alone). But parents' thoughts and perceptions on official guidance and social norms are important. A 2016 study in Victoria found parents were more likely to restrict their child's independent mobility if they were worried about being judged by others. However, the biggest barrier to more parents letting their children walk or ride to school alone is parental concern about speeding cars and other traffic dangers. This is followed by fears around "stranger danger" and abduction (although statistically speaking, kids are much safer on the street than online). It's understandable — the urge to keep kids safe is hardwired in parents. But when we choose to drive to school, we only add to the real traffic dangers and risks even as we continue to frame it as a problem created by others. Or as a legendary outdoor poster by Dutch satnav maker TomTom proclaimed in 2010: "You are not stuck in traffic. You are traffic."

Adapted from https://www.abc.net.au/news/2020-10-20/walk-to-school-children-transport-traffic-health-safety/12660300

Task 1 *Read the article and analyze why parents are more likely to drive their kids to school than let kids go by themselves. You can refer to the information in the article. Jot down the key points in the following box, you should speak for at least 90 seconds.*

Task 2 *Please list the pros and cons of driving kids to school. Give details for each main point and fill the form below.*

Pros of Driving Kids to School	Cons of Driving Kids to School

Task 3   *Should children rely on their parents or be independent? You can use the information from the article as evidence to support your claim.*

1. Your opinion   2. The reasons

Task 4   *Listen to a lecture about "Family Education" and fill the following table according to what you hear.*

Three Ways Children Learn Social Behavior from Their Families	Details
1.	
2.	
3.	

Task 5   *Make a mini debate with the motion — rewards are better than punishments in children cultivation. You may jot down the evidence in the following box.*

Preposition Side	Opposition Side

Task 6 *Please share your idea with your partners about one of the following statements.*

1. Talent cultivation should be the process of educating people of morality and people of ability, among which nurturing people of morality is the basis.

2. Education serves as inheriting the past, forging the present and creating the future, which is the major force to push human civilization forward.

3. Feelings of worth can flourish only in an atmosphere where individual differences are appreciated, mistakes are tolerated, communication is open, and rules are flexible — the kind of atmosphere that is found in a nurturing family.

4. Families are the compass that guides us. They are the inspiration to reach great heights, and our comfort when we occasionally falter.

5. The family you come from isn't as important as the family you're going to have.

6. A father's goodness is higher than the mountain, a mother's goodness deeper than the sea.

7. If you have never been hated by your child you have never been a parent.

8. You have a life time to work, but children are only young once.

Part Six   Encountering IELTS Speaking

Words and Expressions about Family and Children

nuclear family 两代同堂的家庭

extended family 三代、四代甚至五代同堂的家庭，大家庭

three generations living under the same roof 三代同堂

filial duty 子女的义务

dutiful/ filial 忠实的，顺从的，守本分的，恭敬的，孝敬的

the elderly/senior citizens 老年人

the aging is a social problem 人口老龄化是一个社会问题

bed-ridden 卧床不起

their health is declining 他们的健康每况愈下

be paralyzed 瘫痪，麻痹

sit in a wheelchair/move around in a wheelchair 坐轮椅

nursing one's sick parents 照料生病的父母

nursing home 老人院

social welfare 社会福利

be financially independent 经济独立

be retired 退休

pensioner 领养老金者；抚恤金领取者；领年金者

do not want to be regarded as a burden 不想被当作负担

live an isolated life 与世隔绝

live apart from children 不跟孩子一起住

spend one's remaining days happily 颐养天年

fulfil the responsibility of bringing up the young and taking care of the old 尽养育孩子和赡养老人的义务

the generation gap 代沟

be widowed 寡居

widow/widower 寡妇

life expectancy 平均寿命 (=expectation of life)

have a family of one's own 拥有自己的家庭

be pregnant 怀孕

on maternity leave 休产假

give birth to a baby 生孩子

take a baby to the kindergarten 送孩子去幼儿园

breadwinner 养家活口的人

make ends meet 收支相抵，收支平衡

provide financial and emotional support to the young parental abuse 虐待父母

ill-treat/maltreat 虐待，滥用

overpopulation 人口过剩

population density 人口密度

be thickly/sparsely populated 人口稠密 / 稀少

the population is aging 人口老龄化

baby boom 生育高峰

average life span 平均寿命

birth rate 出生率

death rate/mortality rate 死亡率

census 人口调查；户口调查

one-child policy 一对夫妻只生一个孩子

birth control 计划生育

population control 人口控制

population explosion 人口爆炸

marital status 婚姻状况

single/married/divorced 单身 / 结婚 / 离婚

a partner/spouse 夫 / 妻；配偶的一方

matchmaker/go-between 媒人

marriage on the basis of romantic love 自由恋爱结婚

fall in love with sb. at first sight 一见钟情

wedding 婚礼

bride/bridegroom 新娘 / 新郎

the best man 伴郎

maid of honor 伴娘

be divorced 离婚

separated 分居

single parent family 单亲家庭

a broken family 破碎的家庭

get custody of a child 获得对孩子的监护权

alimony (离婚或分居后在诉讼期间男方给女方的) 赡养费，生活费

pay alimony to the wife 为妻子提供赡养费

impact on the child 影响孩子

（household）chores 家庭杂务；日常零星工作

housework 家务 , 劳动 , 家务事

do the laundry 洗 / 熨

washing 要洗的衣物；洗好的衣物

cleaning 清洁（处理），清洗

vacuum 用真空吸尘器打扫

vacuum （cleaner）吸尘器

tidy and neat 整洁

in a mess 混乱，脏乱

get on one's nerves 令人不安

special training 特别训练

vacation jobs 假期工作

refresher courses 进修课程

IELTS Speaking Skill — Main Idea + Supporting Details (deductive pattern)

The major point that IELTS Examiners want to see is a presentation of main ideas and then development by "extension and support."

In the Speaking exam it's important to extend answers as much as possible. By developing an idea, you are giving the examiner a clearer evidence that you can fully answer the question and present your ideas coherently.

Good linking phrases are like clear signposts that help you easily navigate a new town or city. They clearly tell examiner exactly what kind of idea you are presenting.

Example 1

What are your favorite colors?

I love red, because it's the color of love. I guess green is also okay, but I still prefer red. Actually, all my clothes are red.

Example 2

Which relatives did you see most often when you were a child?

I used to see my grandparents four or five times a week because I went there after school when my parents were still at work but I don't see them as often now. Actually, I miss their company a lot so I'm planning to go round more often in the future.

Example 3

What kind of films do you like?

It depends, if I want some excitement, I'll see a horror movie, but if I've had a hard day, I might watch a comedy. Actually, I chose to watch a comedy last night so I guess yesterday was a hard day.

Task   *Please tell your partner your favorite gift in your childhood by using deductive pattern. You can use the linking phrases underlined in the Sample Answers above. You can jot down key words in the following box.*

IELTS Speaking Test Items

Part 1

1. What do you like to do together as a family?
2. Do you have a large or small family?
3. How much time do you spend with your family?
4. Do you get along well with your family?
5. Is yours a typical family?
6. Are there many different types of family in your country?
7. Who are you closest to in your family?
8. Should we rely heavily on our families or is it better to try to be independent?
9. Describe the room you live in?
10. What do you like about living there?

▶ Sample Answer

3. How much time do you spend with your family?

   I usually try to spend most of the time with my family. But I cannot manage time when I am out for my university. But after my return from the university, I do not make any late to share the day-long events with the family members, especially with my mom.

4. Do you get along well with your family?

   Yes, I get very well with my family members. They are supportive, positive, intelligent and caring. I would not say that we never had any disagreement but that's usually momentary. Love is stronger among us and that conquers any misunderstanding that might arrive among us. In fact, I am happy to be a part of such a wonderful family. They love me as much I love them.

Part 2

1. Describe a book you have recently read.
   You should say:
   What type of book it was;
   What it was about;
   Where you read it;
   And how you felt about the book.

I enjoy reading but I don't consider myself as a bookworm, I just read for the sake of learning something new which can be helpful to my profession. Well, I love to spend my time reading educational books.

Just yesterday, while I was enjoying my leisure time, I decided to read a book titled *Teaching Strategies in The Age of Internet* which is authored by a well-known educator in our country. As I am a high school teacher, I got intrigued about the title of the book since it's very timely and I had the feeling that I needed to read it knowing that my students are really hard to deal with.

Well, I had known this book for long as it's advertised in an education magazine, but I never had the chance to get one since I didn't have enough time to go to a bookstore due to my hectic schedule. Luckily a week ago, one of my friends gifted this to me on my birthday. I was thrilled to see it as one of my birthday presents. My friend was like a mind-reader, I didn't tell anyone that I had so much interest of this book and unexpectedly I got hold of it!

Anyway, this education book is approximately 300-pages and what I love about it is the fact that, it's very comprehensive. All the teaching methods that teachers need to know about dealing with millennial students are thoroughly explained. I started reading this book since three days ago at home and I couldn't be happier to know the specific teaching strategies written on this book.

One of the unconventional teaching techniques that caught my attention from that book is that, teachers need to take advantage of the social media craze among students. Teachers should utilize social media in delivering lessons from time to time since students are addicted to using it. We teachers should go with the trend to make the students get engaged in learning.

Thanks to this book, I've become open-minded on how I could better my style of teaching that would surely make my millennial students get more interested in learning.

2. Describe a photograph in your room that you like.

You should say:

What it is;

Where it was taken;

How you got it;

And explain why you like it.

▶ **Sample Answer**

My room is not spacious and I'm the kind of person who finds beauty in minimalism, so I only have a couple of photographs displayed in my room as I avoid overcrowding it with many kinds of photos. One of them and which I must say my ultimate favorite is a portrait of my father when he was only a teenager.

My mom gave it to me when I turned thirteen many years ago as one of her birthday presents. In that photo, my dad looked so handsome in his dominance smile, which I think is one of the reasons why my mom fell in love with him during their high school days. My dad wore his neat and tidy school uniform when he was taken that photograph. My mom told me that the photo was taken for their yearbook. Their teacher gave them a copy of their photographs before publishing their yearbook.

According to my mom, they exchanged their photos with each other and each of them kept it in their wallet as a sign of keeping and treasuring their love. That was so sweet when I heard the story of dad's photograph. He must be a loving and sweet man! Actually, I don't have so many memories of my dad since he died young serving our country.

As what I learned from my dad, he was sent to a remote area in our country together with his troops and fought against the enemies of the state but unfortunately became one of the servicemen who drew their last breath. I was only one and a half years old when he left us, although, I don't have memories with him, I still am very proud of him for what he did to our country and I'm forever grateful for the life he had given me. So, this portrait of my father is for me the best gift in the world and the best photograph of all the photos I have kept as it has a sentimental value to me — this is more than special that I truly hold dear.

3. Describe a goal you once set and tried your best to achieve.

You should say:

When you set the goal;

What it was;

What you did to achieve it;

And explain how you felt about it.

Part 3

1. Which are more important to you: your family or your friends?

2. What are the advantages and disadvantages of taking photos using a smartphone?

3. Do you think art should be sold or preserved?

4. In what ways have families in your country changed recently?

5. Do old and young people like the same holidays?

6. Do young people in your country work longer hours now than in the past?

7. What are the differences between films and books?

8. What are the differences between writing a letter and writing a text message on a phone?

9. Do young and older people use phones in the same way?

10. Is it good for children to learn art at school?

11. Should children learn to play musical instruments?

12. How can we improve children's intelligence?

13. Is it important that children do a variety of sports?

14. For those smart children, are they born to be smart or they are nurtured to be smart?

▶ Sample Answer

6. Do young people in your country work longer hours now than in the past?

I think young people do have to work longer and harder hours these days, and I think that's because the cost of living has become more expensive while salaries have stayed more or less the same. In the past, if you had a part-time or minimum wage job, an adult could still afford their rent and pay their bills. Whereas, nowadays, I've seen that more and more young people have been working multiple jobs in order to make ends meet. So, I think they do work longer hours.

9. Do young and older people use phones in the same way?

I don't think so because the young generation have grown up with modern technology like smartphones, so as a result, they take full advantage of all the newest features and functions, like camera filters, video chatting and instant messaging, whereas the older generation tend to use only the most basic features of a phone, such as phone calls or text messages. That's probably because it's more similar to the technology that they grew up with. So those are some differences I've noticed.

Checklist for This Chapter

Please check according to the scale from 1 to 5.

(1 — Strongly Disagree; 2 — Disagree; 3 — Undecided; 4 —Agree; 5 — Strongly Agree)

Can-do List	1	2	3	4	5
I can describe an object.					
I can compare and contrast two things/ items.					
I can develop answers by using deductive pattern.					
I know the significance of scientific educational notion.					

Self-reflection

1. In which part have I done very well?

2. In which part should I make improvement?

3. What should I do to bridge the current gap?

4. What suggestions do I have for my teacher or the class arrangement?

5. Anything I would like to say.

(Your reflection could be written in Chinese)

CHAPTER 7

Festivals and Traditions

LEARNING OBJECTIVES

In this chapter you will learn

- how to structure an answer to the topic of event
- how to use discourse markers to describe an event
- how to give solutions to a problem
- how to use paraphrasing strategy in IELTS Speaking Test
- the value of appreciating diverse cultures and customs

Part One   Warming-up

Task 1   *Discuss in pairs. What is the festival in each picture below? Which is the festival you enjoy most? Jot down the key words in the following box.*

A

B

C

D

E   F

Task 2 *Discuss in pairs. When do people do the activities below? Choose the activity you enjoy most and give reasons. Are there any other activities that you would like to participate in during festivals?*

let off fireworks   go to the temple fair   make Zongzi

carve pumpkin lanterns   post couplets on doors   guess lantern riddles

The activity I enjoy most

Reasons

Other activities

Task 3 *Please list some traditions of celebrating New Year in your country and western countries. You may discuss with your partners and share your discussion results with other groups.*

Traditions in Your Country	Traditions in Western Countries

Part Two   IELTS Speaking Test

IELTS Speaking Skill — Description of an Event

Events and experiences are usually talked about in IELTS Speaking Test Part 2, which account for more than 30% of the total questions in 2021.

The classification of topics about events are as follow.

■ **Topics about personal experience**

   a recent happy event that you had
   a short trip that was special to you
   a family event from your childhood
   a mistake that you once made
   a situation that you got a little angry
   an occasion when you got up early
   an activity that you do in your school
   an occasion you remember that you met someone for the first time
   an occasion when the weather changed your plan

■ **Topics about the embodiment of something abstract**

a good decision you made recently

a positive change in your life

a useful advice you have received

an important stage of your life

■ **Topics about festival/historical events**

a tradition in your country

a historical event you know

an important festival in your country

When talking about an event, you can structure your answer by three parts — before the event, during the event and after the event. More details about the contents are shown below.

Before the event	Background of the event	Why it happened
	Preparation for the event	How people prepare for the event
During the event	Description of the event	When it happened Where it happened Who were there What happened
	A special detail about the event	What impressed you most
After the event	Feelings and gain	How you feel about it What you learned from it

In the IELTS Speaking Test band descriptors(Table 7-1), the usage of connectives and discourse markers is part of the criteria as shown below.

Table 7-1   IELTS Speaking Test Band Descriptors (Excerpt)

Band	Descriptors
5	may over-use certain connectives and discourse markers
6	uses a range of connectives and discourse markers but not always appropriately
7	uses a range of connectives and discourse markers with some flexibility

Discourse markers

■ Introduction of the talk

I'm going to talk about ... (, which ...)

The event I would like to talk about is ...

■ Introduction of a new point

In terms of ...

As to/ As for ...

When it comes to ...

What impressed me most is that ...

The reason why ...is that ...

I have to say I really felt ...

I learned a lot from the experience.

■ Time or logical sequence

First, / Firstly, / First of all, ...

To begin with, ...

To start with, ...

Second, / Secondly, ...

Third, / Thirdly, ...

In addition, ...

As well as that, ...

Besides, ...

Lastly, ...

Finally, ...

- Giving examples

  For example, ...

  For instance, ...

  In particular, ...

  Such as ...

- Explanation or giving details

  That is to say, ...

  In other words, ...

  Actually, ...

  As a matter of fact, ...

  In fact, ...

- Making comparisons

  However, ...

  On the other hand, ...

  While ...

  Whereas ...

- The end of the talk

  Those are the reasons why ...

  So this is the experience that ...

Task 1 *Think about a time when you were excited. Plan your ideas about this exciting event. Talk with your partner about the exciting event. You can use the discourse markers provided to help you.*

Before the event	Background of the event	
	Preparation for the event	
During the event	Description of the event	
	A special detail about the event	
After the event	Feelings and gain	

Please share your idea with your partners about the following questions. Use proper discourse markers in your speaking.

1. What are the differences between traditional festivals and new festivals?
2. Do you think it is important to preserve traditional festivals?

Part Three   Speaking after Reading

The Origins and History of Gift Giving

Gift giving has been a long tradition that dates back thousands of years as far back as man can remember. As human beings, we are social creatures who enjoy each other's company and expressing our feelings through the giving of gifts. Whether it is an expression of true love, appreciation of a job well done or just to show our gratitude for having someone as a friend, the giving of gifts is engrained into our DNA.

Origins of gift giving

The giving of gifts may be one of the oldest of human traditions that pre-dates civilization and may go back to the origin of our species. Even in primitive cavemen culture, the giving of gifts was fairly common as it was used to show love and affection towards one another. The bestowing of gifts was also inferred as a status symbol when leaders of tribes or clans would show their appreciation for the contributions of those who were part of an important achievement.

Later during the Egyptian era, gifts were most notably given to their pharaohs who built massive pyramids to store their wealth for afterlife and produced idols to support their beliefs of idol worship. In Roman times people would present each other with good luck tokens, which lasted for centuries and later influenced all of Western civilization onwards.

By the Medieval age, gifts were used to secure the personal favor of the king or show allegiance in times of war. Also, personal gifts of betrothals were given as dowries which ranged from coins to precious metals to a herd of cattle, goats or sheep.

Today gift giving is still part of our everyday culture and defines who we are and the message we want to send with our gift. Gifts are given for all occasions and celebrations and are a means of us communicating with each other and expressing ourselves.

The psychology behind gift giving

Today, gift giving is a tradition that spreads across all cultures around the world, and the psychology of why gift giving is so rewarding is simple — it allows people to connect. The giver of a gift expresses their feelings and emotions by sending a gift with the hope of being able to share these with the receiver of the gift. The receiver of the gift in turn receives the feelings and emotions and with this a connection is made. Making connections with people around us gives us a sense of purpose and feeling of satisfaction. This feeling is one that enlightens the soul and brings out the best in us. There is an old saying "it is better to give than receive" and it has a special meaning especially when the realization of the benefits that it provides to those who give.

Why is it important to give gifts?

There has been a considerable amount of research over the years into the feelings of wellbeing that occurs when we give gifts to those we care about. From as early as cavemen days gift giving has been rewarding, which may be the reason why it has stood the test of time and become a long and continuous tradition. Here are some reasons as to why:

We Feel Happy: Simply put, the giving of gifts can make a person feel happier about themselves as well as to the person that has received their gift.

Improve State of Mind: Research suggests that giving gifts may improve a person's state of mind. If giving a gift makes you feel happier with a sense of purpose then this may inevitably improve your state of mind.

Greater Social Connection: By giving a gift, you are not only expressing your feelings but building a stronger connection to that person as well. Not only does the person receiving the gift feel closer to the giver, but vice versa as well. This greater social connection also means an improvement in the state of being as well as overall happiness.

It's Contagious: When a person starts giving gifts, not only will the recipient become more likely to give, those around them who see this act will start giving as well. This is in part due to the release of the endorphins, which not only benefits the giver, but is also felt by those who receive and see the act of giving as well.

Adapted from the internet- https://www.curioushistory.com/the-origins-and-history-of-gift-giving

Word Bank

gratitude	*n.* being thankful 感激，感谢
engrain	*v.* firmly fix or establish (a habit, belief, or attitude) in a person 使根深蒂固
civilization	*n.* the stage of human social development and organization which is considered most advanced 文明；文化
caveman	*n.* a prehistoric man who lived in caves 史前石器时代的穴居人
affection	*n.* a gentle feeling of fondness or liking 喜爱
bestow	*v.* confer of present (an honour, right, or gift) 授予；使用
clan	*n.* a close-knit group of interrelated families 宗族；部落
pharaoh	*n.* a ruler in ancient Egypt 法老
pyramid	*n.* a monumental structure with a square or triangular base and sloping sides that meet in a point at the top, especially one built of stone as a royal tomb in ancient Egypt 金字塔
afterlife	*n.* life after death 过世后
worship	*v.* show reverence and adoration for (a deity) 崇拜；礼拜
token	*n.* a voucher that can be exchanged for goods or services 代币
allegiance	*n.* loyalty 忠诚；拥护
betrothal	*n.* engagement 订婚
dowry	*n.* an amount of property or money brought by a bride to her husband on their marriage 嫁妆
psychology	*n.* the mental characteristics or attitude 心理
enlighten	*v.* give greater knowledge and understanding 启发；开导
wellbeing	*n.* the state of being comfortable, healthy, or happy 康乐；安康
vice versa	*adv.* with the main items in the preceding statement the other way round 反过来也一样
contagious	*adj.* (an emotion, feeling, or attitude) likely to spread to and affect others 有感染力的
recipient	*n.* a person or thing that receives or is awarded something 接受者

Read the article and pick up the best choice.

1. When did people present others with good luck tokens as a gift?

    A) Egyptian era.

    B) Medieval age.

    C) Roman times.

    D) cavemen days.

2. What were commonly used as gifts of engagement in ancient times?

    A) Metals, jewels, animals.

    B) Metals, animals, coins.

    C) Animals, coins, jewels.

    D) Metals, jewels, coins.

3. From a psychological perspective, what is the reason why giving gifts is an advantageous behavior?

    A) It creates an emotional connection between the giver and the receiver of gifts.

    B) The receiver of gifts would feel he or she is valued.

    C) The giver of gifts can always be rewarded.

    D) The giver of gifts may have a sense of superiority.

4. Which is the main reason why the action of giving gifts become contagious?

    A) The production of a hormone creates benefits to many people.

    B) Giving gifts is a way to show off wealth.

    C) Giving gifts may improve a person's state of mind.

    D) The giver of a gift is happier than the receiver.

Task 2 *Please share ideas with your partners about the following questions based on what you read.*

1. What is the purpose of giving gifts in primitive culture?

2. What is the purpose of giving gifts in modern life?

3. What are the reasons why gift giving continues and even becomes a tradition?

4. What gifts do you want to have most for your next birthday? Why?

5. What gifts do you want to give to your parents? Why?

Task 3 *Please retell the following short paragraph by using your own words.*

By giving a gift, you are not only expressing your feelings but building a stronger connection to that person as well. Not only does the person receiving the gift feel closer to the giver, but vice versa as well. This greater social connection also means an improvement in the state of being as well as overall happiness.

Task 4 *Please make a survey among your peers and report the result of your survey in class. You are recommended to do the survey with your group members. The following questions may be included in your survey.*

1. When do they give gifts to others?
2. Who do they usually send gifts to?
3. What is the gift that they want to receive most?
4. How do they feel when giving a gift to others and receiving a gift from others?
5. Are there any differences between giving gifts to the elder and the young?
6. What gifts you want to send to your foreign friends?

Part Four   Speaking after Listening

IELTS Speaking Skill — Problem-Solution

When a problem need to be dealt with, you need to provide some ways to solve it. You can use the following expressions when giving solutions.

> Actually, there are plenty of ways to do ...
> Well, there are a great many things we can do to ...
> I believe a lot of measures could be taken to address this problem. ...
> Well, several steps could be taken. ...
> Well, measures to this problem are various. ...
> What we can do to solve this problem is that ...
> In order to solve this problem, ...
> Well, based on the disadvantages of this issue, I think there are some effective methods to deal with the situation. ...

In terms of problem-solution questions, solutions are usually given from different levels or fields. For example, something can be done on both personal level and social level, or you can also consider measures from the perspective of government, companies as well as individuals. It is an effective way to extend your answer.

When you have more than one measure, some logical connectors can be added between sentences.

First, ...
Firstly, ...
First of all, ...
I guess the top priority is ...
The most effective way would be ...

Then, ...
Next, ...
Besides, ...
Also, ...
In addition, ...
Moreover, ...
What's more, ...
More importantly, ...
As far as ... are concerned, ...

Example

What should be done to help maintain a traditional culture/ festival?

As far as I am concerned, a great many measures could be taken.

Firstly, government should strengthen publicity of important festival and public-service announcements might be an effective method. Some regulations can also be adopted if necessary, such as on the holiday system, coz holiday is a basic guarantee for people to celebrate festival.

Besides, companies and organizations should also take responsibility for the preservation of traditional festival. They should obey the rules and make sure employees have time to spend the festival with their family.

More importantly, every single citizen should recognize the importance of our traditions and do something related to the special days. For instance, when the

Mid-Autumn Festival comes, we shall eat moon cakes and enjoy a reunion dinner with family.

Task 1 *The following items contain important vocabulary from the report—Thanksgiving Features Native American Foods. Work with a partner and match vocabulary terms with their definitions. Check your answers in a dictionary if necessary.*

_____ 1. Many of the traditional foods eaten at Thanksgiving dinner have Native American roots but have been **spiced** up.

_____ 2. He's on a team that put together the **cafeteria's** menu at the Museum of the American Indian in Washington D.C.

_____ 3. Chef Hetzler points out that Native Americans taught the European settlers how to **trap**, gather, and preserve the food that allowed them to survive in North America.

_____ 4. Hetzler says **a wide array** of Native American foods would have been present at the first Thanksgiving.

_____ 5. Chef Hetzler has tried to take the **bland** ingredients in Native American foods and adapt them to the modern palate.

_____ 6. Chef Hetzler has tried to take the bland ingredients in Native American foods and adapt them to the modern **palate**.

_____ 7. So they would have cut them and laid them out in the sun. And then they would have **reconstituted** them in soups and things of that nature.

a. build up again from parts

b. a wide range of

c. a restaurant in which customers serve themselves from a counter and pay before eating

d. sense of taste

e. enhance the taste by adding a particular ingredient

f. lacking strong features or characteristics

g. catch something

Task 2 *Listen to a talk about "Thanksgiving Features: Native American Foods", and choose the best answer according to have you have heard.*

1. How many regions did Richard Hetzler and his team collect menu from?

   A) 3   B) 4   C) 5   D) 6

2. According to the description of Hetzler, why did Native Americans want to give thanks at this specific time of a year?

A) They were able to go hunting at this time.

B) A new leader was usually chosen at this time.

C) It is the time when they could immigrate to other area.

D) It is the time when they had the most sufficient food.

3. What are the ingredients of "Three Sister Salad"?

A) cabbage, squash, beans

B) corn, squash, beans

C) corn, cabbage, beans

D) corn, cabbage, squash

4. What characteristic of bread met the demand of carrying food for Native Americans?

A) It was very small.

B) It was very light.

C) It was very dense.

D) It had special shape.

5. What is the most important skill that European settlers learned from Native Americans?

A) how to farm

B) how to make tools for transport

C) how to build a sturdy house

D) how to preserve food

6. What was first used by settlers for different purposes?

A) salt   B) cooker   C) oil   D) bowl

Task 3   *Please paraphrase the following sentence by using your own words.*

But the friendship between the settlers and the Native Americans did not last long. Eventually, European settlers drove the Native Americans off their lands. And the settlers lost touch with many Native American foods ... except on Thanksgiving.

Task 4   *Please discuss with your partners about the following questions. Try to use the skill of problem-solution discussed in the previous part. You can do peer or self-evaluation by using the criteria below.*

1. How to keep food fresh?

2. What do you think we can do to preserve traditional food?

3. What do you think are effective ways to develop healthy eating habits?

4. How to balance flavor and nutrition of dishes?

Criteria for Peer- / Self-Assessment

NO.	Analytic Items	Proportion	Peer- /Self-Assessment
1	Using the expressions of problem-solving	20%	
2	Fluency (less accidental pauses, short pause length, less self-correction)	20%	
3	Accuracy (accuracy in using words and expressions, accuracy in grammar use)	20%	
4	Complexity(lexical variety, usage of less frequent vocabulary, syntactic complexity)	20%	
5	Pronunciation (no strong accent, correct stress, liaison, plosion in words and sentences, sounds naturally)	20%	
Total Score (use a 10-point scale)			

Part Five   Critical Thinking

The Chinese and the Moon

The traditional Mid-Autumn Festival enjoys great popularity in China where it is second only to the Spring Festival, or Chinese New Year, and in some of its neighboring countries.

The Mid-Autumn Festival falls on the 15th day of the eighth lunar month. Since ancient times, people have celebrated it by worshipping and admiring the glorious full moon, and the Chinese believe that the full moon represents family reunions. Therefore, Mid-

Autumn Festival is also a day for families to get together and for those far away from home to think of their loved ones.

Legend of Chang'e

The origin of the festival goes back to the legend of a beautiful woman called Chang'e. According to Chinese historic records, Chang'e was the wife of Houyi, an archer who was once granted an elixir of immortality for his heroic acts. One day, when Houyi was not at home, Chang'e drank the elixir, which then made her fly upward towards the sky, but as she loved her husband and hoped to live close to him, she choose the Moon as her new home. Upon discovering that Chang'e was not going to come back, to relieve the sorrow of losing his wife, Yi set out various fruits and cakes that Chang'e liked in the garden underneath the Moon, and did so every 15th day of every 8th lunar month of each year, as that was the day when Chang'e was carried away to the Moon. As for Chang'e, she found herself all alone on the Moon, except for a Jade Rabbit who crafted the beverage for immortality all year round. Since then, a custom evolved in which people would worship the Moon on the day of Mid-Autumn — the 15th day of the 8th lunar month.

Mid-Autumn Festival customs

At Mid-Autumn Festival, a memorial tablet to the Moon Goddess is set up in each household with fruits, melons and mooncakes placed in front of it as a sacrifice. The cake must be round and melons and fruits are cut into lotus-petal-shaped pieces. Some people also buy joss paper with images of the Goddess and patterns like the Jade Rabbit making heavenly medicine printed on it. After the moon-worshipping ceremony, people burn the joss paper and family members share the fruits and moon cakes. At the festival of family reunion, people give each other mooncakes as gifts to express their good wishes.

Apart from the common traditions, different regions also have their unique customs and celebrations on this day. For people in East China's Zhejiang Province, tidal bore watching is an important event on this day when the most spectacular tides are formed in the Qiantang River. Its turbulent waves can sometimes reach several meters in height, overwhelming everything in their way, like herds of stampeding horses.

In Guangzhou, on Mid-Autumn night, kids fix different shaped lanterns on short sticks that are then positioned vertically one by one on a high pole. These splendidly glittering lights, add a new beauty to the festival. Kids enjoy racing to be the first to erect the highest pole hung with the most exquisite and largest number of lamps.

In Nanning, Guangxi Zhuang Autonomous Region, people also have a tradition of making lamps with bamboo strips that are hung in front of a moon-worshipping table. Kids also play with these lamps. In addition, lamps made from grapefruit, orange peel and pumpkin are also popular during this festival.

Flying to the moon

The name of Chang'e was chosen for the remarkable Chinese lunar program. On November 24, 2020, China launched Chang'e 5, a large robotic spacecraft, at the Wenchang Space Launch Center in South China's Hainan province, tasking it with landing on the moon and bringing back lunar samples, 44 years after the last time such extraterrestrial substances were brought back to Earth.

According to a statement published by the space administration, the Chang'e 5 mission is intended to fulfill several objectives. In terms of space engineering, it will demonstrate and verify technical plans and apparatus for autonomous lunar sampling and packing, and moon-based launching, as well as lunar orbital docking. In the scientific field, it will investigate the landing site's geological and topographic features, and enable scientists to analyze the lunar samples' structure and physical traits so they can deepen their research into the moon's origin and evolution.

Adapted and edited from *China Daily, China Today*, and the Internet resources,
https://eastant.it/cn/index.php?m=&c=Index&a=show&catid=4&id=135

Task 1 *Read the article and introduce the origin of Mid-Autumn Festival to your partners by using your own words. You can refer to the information in the article. You may jot down the key points in the following box.*

Task 2 *Please illustrate common traditions in China and unique customs in different regions during to Mid-Autumn Festival. Give details for each main point and fill the form below.*

1	Common Traditions	
2	Zhejiang Province	
3	Guangzhou	
4	Nanning, Guangxi Zhuang Autonomous Region	

Task 3 *Talk about the customs of Mid-Autumn Festival in your home town and tell your partner which one you enjoy most and explain why.*

1. The customs in my home town:

2. The custom I enjoy most:

3. The reason:

Task 4 *Listen to a lecture about "Spooky Halloween" and fill the following sentences according to what you hear.*

1. The festival, also called All Hallows' Eve or All Hallows' Evening, which means to remember the dead, has gradually developed into _____, and has become one of the most popular festivals among children and adults with its _____.

2. Families in Chile, meanwhile, visit the _____ and place _____ to _____ of their loved ones.

3. Another go-to place for _____ is Yiwu, the world's largest _____ where _____ from all over the world _____.

4. Parents were asked to prepare costumes and _____ for their

children and attend the _____ in school.

5. While some treat it as a _____ between parents and children, others complain that it has gone too far.

6. Instead of treating Western festivals as _____, the bigger question is how to keep the traditional culture _____ amid the _____ world.

Task 5   *Listen to the lecture again and choose the best answer according to what you have heard.*

1. Which description is a Halloween custom of Germany?
    A) watch costume play
    B) decorate tombs with flowers
    C) watching horror films
    D) celebrate it from October 31 to November 2

2. Which region is not mentioned to import products from the company in Shenyang?
    A) Europe
    B) Southeast Asia
    C) Australia
    D) America

3. How much stuff that is used to celebrate important holidays in the world is from Yiwu?
    A) 50%
    B) 60%
    C) 70%
    D) 80%

4. Which factor contributes to the popularity of Western festivals?
    A) Western festivals are weird.
    B) Western festivals are more interesting.
    C) Western festivals have more lively atmosphere.
    D) Western festivals are suitable for young people and old people.

Task 6   *Talk with your partners about your attitudes toward festivals of foreign countries. Why do you think people, especially the young, prefer to celebrate foreign festivals? You can jot down the key points in the following box.*

Task 7 *Please share your idea with your partners about one of the following statements.*

1. Science and technology revolutionize our lives, but memory, tradition and myth frame our response.

2. We must be in tune with the times and prepared to break with tradition.

3. Artificial intelligence is destroying the traditional world of work.

4. Tradition can, to be sure, participate in a creation, but it can no longer be creative itself.

Part Six   Encountering IELTS Speaking

Words and Expressions about Festival and Traditions

New Year's Day 元旦

the Spring Festival 春节

New Year's Eve 除夕

the Lantern Festival 元宵节

the Dragon Boat Festival 端午节

the Army's Day 建军节

the Mid-Autumn Festival 中秋节

the Double Ninth Day 重阳节

Valentine's Day 情人节

Double-Seventh Day 七夕

Tomb-sweeping Day 清明节

Laba Festival 腊八节

April Fools' Day 愚人节

International Children's Day 儿童节

Teacher's Day 教师节

National Day 国庆节

Easter Day 复活节

Halloween 万圣节前夜

Thanksgiving Day 感恩节

Christmas Day 圣诞节

Mother's Day 母亲节

Father's Day 父亲节

International Labour Day 国际劳动节

World No-Smoking Day 世界无烟日

World Earth Day 世界地球日

religious festivals 宗教节日

non-religious festivals 非宗教节日

traditional customs 传统风俗

teach traditional skills 教授传统技艺

traditional values 传统价值

cultural heritage 文化遗产

cultural identity 文化特性

ethnic minorities 少数民族

Spring Festival Gala 春晚

crosstalk 相声

firecracker 鞭炮

fireworks 烟花

red envelope / red packet 红包

exile 放逐

loyal minister 忠臣

dragon boat races 龙舟比赛

play the lion dance 耍狮子

play the dragon lantern 耍龙灯

pay a new-year call 拜年

traditional costumes 传统服饰

skilled craftsmen 手工艺人

hand-made goods 手工制品

cheongsam 旗袍

embroidery 刺绣

paper cutting 剪纸

calligraphy 书法

couplet 对联

seal 印章

Chinese knot 中国结

shadow puppets 皮影

riddle 谜语

acupuncture 针灸

lunar calendar 农历

five elements 五行

be matched for marriage 门当户对

wedding and funeral 红白喜事

symbolic significance 象征意义

sweet dumpling 元宵

spring roll 春卷

eight-treasure rice pudding 八宝饭

steamed bun 小笼包

pastry 糕点

fried bread stick 油条

soybean milk 豆浆

tea egg 茶叶蛋

bean paste cake 绿豆糕

porridge 粥

hot pot 火锅

Peking duck 北京烤鸭

Dongpo pork 东坡肉

lotus root 莲藕

snack stand 小吃摊

Peking opera 京剧

Shaanxi opera 秦腔

Kunqu opera 昆曲

Shaoxing opera 越剧

Huangmei opera 黄梅戏

flower drum opera 花鼓戏

Er ren zhuan 二人转

puppet show 木偶戏

Confucian culture 儒家文化

Confucius 孔子

Mencius 孟子

Tai Chi 太极拳

the four treasures of the study 文房四宝

brush, ink stick, paper, and inkstone 笔墨
纸砚

oracle bone inscription 甲骨文

hieroglyphic 象形文字

radical 偏旁

the Great Wall 长城

Temple of Heaven 天坛

Old Summer Palace 圆明园

the Summer Palace 颐和园

The Palace Museum 故宫博物院

Buddhist temple 佛寺

beacon tower 烽火台

Hutong 胡同

Siheyuan / courtyard 四合院

Loess Plateau　黄土高原

Terracotta Warriors　兵马俑

tri-coloured glazed pottery of the Tang Dynasty　唐三彩

costume film　古装片

Chinese Swordplay Movie　武打片

Chinese zither　古筝

Erhu　二胡

The Book of Songs　《诗经》

The Dream of Red Mansion　《红楼梦》

Journey to the West　《西游记》

Water Margin　《水浒传》

Romance of the Three Kingdoms　《三国演义》

Historical Records　《史记》

Compendium of Materia Medica　《本草纲目》

old-fashioned　过时的

variation　变化

IELTS Speaking Skill — Paraphrase

What does paraphrase mean?

The verb paraphrase means to sum something up or clarify a statement by rephrasing it. So to paraphrase that explanation, it means to say something in other, simpler words.

If you break paraphrase down, you end up with the prefix para, meaning "beside," and the word phrase — so think of paraphrase as coming up with similar, more simple phrases that go beside the ones already said.

Adapted from https://www. vocabulary.com/dictionary/Paraphrase

Paraphrasing is defined as a faithful restatement of the source text using one's own words. It is an important device in academic writing and speaking. The purpose of paraphrasing is to recast the source text based on the author's own understanding with the expectation that the paraphrased texts can well serve authorial intentions and successfully incorporate into the writing or speaking.

In paraphrasing, the writer or speaker recasts individual sentences, creating a combination of original language and grammatical structures from the source text with some new words and grammatical structures.

There are a few techniques which can be adopted in paraphrasing, like using synonyms, changing word order or sentence order, changing parts of speech of the words in the original text, etc.

视频学习链接：https://www.bilibili.com/video/BV1pq4y1y7DM/

When should we paraphrase?

■ Do not know or do not remember a word

When you do not know the exact word or cannot remember a word in your speaking, you can describe the word in other words.

■ Stop repeating yourself

Some words, especially the key words of the topic, may need to be said for several times in your answer. Paraphrase can help you to reduce the repeat.

■ Paraphrase what the examiner has said

Using different words with your examiner is a demonstration of vocabulary.

How to paraphrase?

■ Description

Use a sentence to describe the original word. Relative clauses are usually effective in the description.

TV remote → The device that we use to control the TV.

■ Synonym

Use another word or phrase that has the same meaning with the original expression.

We should protect the ecological environment. → We should preserve the ecological environment.

■ Antonym

Use another word or phrase that has an opposite meaning with the original expression.

I am free on weekends. → I am not busy on weekends.

■ Different parts of speech

Another part of speech can be utilized to realize the changing of original expression.

Many old people preferred tea. → Many old people have a preference for tea.

■ Different types of voice

A sentence can be converted from active voice to passive voice, and vice versa.

We should protect endangered animals. → Endangered animals should be protected.

In the IELTS Speaking Test band descriptors, paraphrase is part of the criteria as shown in the below table.

Table 7–2   IELTS Speaking Test Band Descriptors (Excerpt)

Band	Descriptors
5	attempts to use *paraphrase* but with mixed success
6	generally *paraphrases* successfully
7	uses *paraphrase* effectively
8	uses *paraphrase* effectively as required

Task 1   *If you had forgotten or did not know the words in bold in these sentences, how would you express them?*

1. The giving of gifts is an expression of true love, or just to show our **gratitude** for having someone as a friend.

2. Giving gifts has become a **global** tradition.

3. I think the biggest thing is that it was truly to give thanks. It was an end of the year when food **harvest**.

4. The traditional Mid-Autumn Festival enjoys great popularity in China where it is second only to the Spring Festival, or Chinese New Year, and in some of its **neighboring** countries.

5. The origin of the festival goes back to the **legend** of a beautiful woman called Chang'e.

Task 2   *Paraphrase the following words and sentences and discuss with your partners about the strategies you use.*

NO.	Original Description	Paraphrasing	Strategies
1	vacuum		
2	a difficult task		
3	The price of the gift is reasonable.		
4	Western holidays become popular because of globalization.		
5	We shouldn't forget traditions in modern society.		

IELTS Speaking Test Items

Part 1

Public holiday

1. How many public holidays do you have in China?

2. Which holiday is your favorite?

3. How do you usually spend your holidays?

4. Do you think people need more public holidays?

Traditional buildings

5. Are there any traditional buildings in your home town?

6. How to preserve traditional buildings?

7. Do you think traditional buildings should be replaced by modern buildings? Why?

Desserts

8. What kind of holidays or festivals require a cake/making a cake?

9. Are there any special cakes?

10. How do people in your country feel about desserts?

▶ **Sample Answer**

1. How many public holidays do you have in China?

   Well, I'm afraid I can't tell the exact number but I think there are at least four, which are the Chinese Spring Festival holiday, Tomb-sweeping Day, Mid-Autumn Festival and National Day holiday. People can get legal holidays for 1 to 7 days to celebrate the important festival.

6. How to preserve traditional buildings?

   Actually, I believe a great many of measures could be taken to protect traditional buildings. Government should allocate more financial budget to the maintenance of these buildings and make use of public service announcements or brochures to improve public awareness of preserving old architecture. Besides, citizens should recognise the importance of traditional buildings and don't destroy them.

10. How do people in your country feel about desserts?

    Well, it's hard to say, since different people may have different tastes. I guess, in terms of dessert, what Chinese people have in common is that we must have a kind of traditional dessert — moon cake on the Mid-Autumn Festival, which is popular not only because of its different fillings, but the meaning of reunion.

Part 2

1. Describe a festival that is important in your country.

   You should say:

   When the festival occurs;

   What you did during it;

   What you like or dislike about it;

   And explain why this festival is important.

▶ **Sample Answer**

When talking about festivals in my country, I would like to say the Dragon Boat Festival is a really important one for Chinese people. It falls on the 5th day of the 5th lunar month, the source of its alternative name, the Double Fifth Festival.

There are many legends about this festival, the most popular of which is in commemoration of the death of Qu Yuan, a Chu state official and poet who lived during the Warring States Period. He was exiled after opposing his king's decision to ally with the neighboring state of Qin, and when Chu was finally conquered by Qin, he committed suicide by drowning himself in the Miluo River on the fifth day of the fifth lunar month.

The local people, who admired this loyal minister, threw balls of sticky rice into the river to feed the fish so they would not eat the body of their hero, which is said to be the origin of Zongzi. Besides, it is said Chu people started dragon boat racing to scare off the fish, as the origin of dragon boat races.

Now Dragon boat racing is an indispensable part of the festival, held all over the country. However, the most enjoyable activity during this festival for me would be making Zongzi, which I learned from my grandma at a very young age. First, we need to take two or three bamboo leaves and make a funnel shape, and then rice and different fillings, such as dates, beans, meats and eggs, are filled into it, after which we need to fold the leaves over and bind with string. A Zongzi is done! I can always get a sense of achievement during this process.

In terms of the importance of this festival, actually, the Dragon Boat Festival is one of the oldest festivals, not only in China but also throughout the world, with a history of more than 2,000 years. It was listed as one of China's national intangible cultural heritages. So I have to say the Dragon Boat Festival is an entertaining, enjoyable and meaningful event.

2. Describe a tradition in your country.
   You should say:
   What the tradition is;
   How it has been preserved;
   What people do for the tradition;
   And explain whether you like or dislike the tradition.

3. Describe a holiday or festival or ceremony from your country.
   You should say:
   When it is celebrated;
   Why it is celebrated;
   How it is celebrated;
   And explain how you feel about the holiday or festival.

4. Describe a (traditional) performance you recently watched.
   You should say:
   What it was;
   When and where you watched it
   Who you were with;
   And explain why you watched it.

Part 3

1. What are some differences between traditional festivals and new festivals?
2. Have the ways people celebrate festivals changed over the past few years?
3. What are some advantages and disadvantages of having a traditional lifestyle?
4. Do young people prefer traditional lifestyles or modern ones?
5. Would you say that foreign festivals like Christmas are replacing traditional festivals in your country?
6. Why should children learn about traditions?
7. What are the differences between online games and traditional games?

▶ **Sample Answer**

1. What are some differences between traditional festivals and new festivals?

   Actually, there are a great many differences, but the most significant one exists in the age group that celebrate these two types of festivals. The population tend to be younger when it comes to the celebration of new festivals, while traditional ones are more preferred by older people. Besides, the ways of celebration are not the same. I mean, people usually company their families in traditional festivals, and Spring Festival would a perfect example for this. On the other hand, friends might be their first choice to hang out together in terms of new festivals, like Strawberry music festival.

2. Have the ways people celebrate festivals changed over the past few years?

   Well, the answer would be both yes and no. Generally speaking, many customs of important festivals are still popular today. For example, people would eat mooncake and admire the moon on the on Mid-Autumn Day, and during Spring Festival, they would have a reunion dinner and let off fireworks. Red packets are given to younger generations. These traditions are still preserved. However, the ways of celebration have also varied in some aspects. Take red envelope for example, grandparents now can give this lucky money to grandchildren via virtual red envelope in Wechat or Alipay, which is actually a payment function in the applications.

Checklist for This Chapter

Please check according to the scale from 1 to 5.

(1 — Strongly Disagree; 2 — Disagree; 3 — Undecided; 4 —Agree; 5 — Strongly Agree)

Can-do List	1	2	3	4	5
I know how to structure an answer to the topic of event.					
I know how to use discourse markers to describe an event.					
I know how to give solutions to a problem.					
I can use paraphrasing strategy in speaking.					
I know the value of appreciating diverse cultures and customs.					

Self-reflection

1. In which part have I done very well?

2. In which part should I make improvement?

3. What should I do to bridge the current gap?

4. What suggestions do I have for my teacher or the class arrangement?

5. Anything I would like to say.

(Your reflection could be written in Chinese)

8

Technology and Innovation

LEARNING OBJECTIVES

In this chapter you will learn

- what the six types of questions in IELTS Speaking Test Part 3 are
- how to use ARS strategy in IELTS Speaking Test
- how to use different evidence to support your opinion
- developing critical thinking on hi-tech innovation
- technological breakthroughs in modern China

Part One   Warming-up

Task 1   *List four situations where AI is involved in your daily life in the following box. Share ideas with your partners.*

1.

2.

3.

4.

Task 2 *Listen to a short presentation about "a brief introduction to artificial intelligence". Complete the sentences using words from the recording.*

1. Artificial intelligence is a broad area of _____ that makes machine seem like they have human intelligence.

2. When it comes to AI, a _____ is nothing more than a _____ concealing what's actually used to _____.

3. AI is expected to become _____ and _____.

4. As AI becomes more intelligent, it will obviously take on the role of an _____ _____ while most of the _____ tasks can be automated using AI.

5. AI is a boon that can help _____, this means that as always, it's not _____, rather it is _____ humans and AI versus the actual problem statement.

Task 3 *Think about the applications of AI in Task 1, and answer the following questions.*

- What problems might AI bring?
- How could humans take precautions against the problems?

Potential Problems of AI	Precautions Against Problems

Part Two   IELTS Speaking Test

Question Types in Part 3 of IELTS Speaking Test

Part 3 is the last part of IELTS Speaking Test. Candidates will talk with the examiner about issues related to the topic on the card of Part 2, but the questions and answers are expected to be more general, focusing on the society rather than personal life.

Although this part may include a variety of questions, in most cases, we can classify these questions into six different categories (see Table 8–1).

Table 8–1   Question Types of IELTS Speakig Test Part 3

NO.	Types of Questions	Examples
1	Opinion	▪ Is it good to use new technology in education? ▪ Do new inventions make people lazy? ▪ Do you think people rely too much on technology?
2	Comparison and contrast	▪ What are differences between men and women on the attitude towards technological devices? ▪ Do you think computers make our life simpler or more complex?
3	Cause and effect	▪ Why do people invent new things? ▪ Why do you think people spend so much money buying the latest devices? ▪ What effect does new technology have on employment?
4	Past and future	▪ Do you think it is possible that robots will replace human labour in the future? ▪ How much has technology improved how we communicate with each other?
5	Advantages and disadvantages	▪ What are the benefits of investing in technology? ▪ What are the possible problems caused by AI?
6	Problem-solution	▪ Could you suggest some solutions to reduce people's reliance on technology? ▪ How could schools use more technology to help children learn?

Is Modern Media Destroying Our Memories?

Although technology may be changing what information we encode, store, and retrieve, it does not appear to be altering our memory machinery.

Here's a question that will only make sense to readers of a certain age: What was your childhood telephone number? I'm guessing you had no problem rattling that off despite not having dialed or recited those digits in decades. If technology were truly killing our memory, then surely this useless bit of information would have faded away long ago. But I submit that modern human beings have the same memory capabilities we've always had; technology is merely redefining how we choose to employ them.

To understand what's going on, we must first become acquainted with the structure of memory. In its simplest form, memory can be understood as a three-step process: first we encode information in the brain; then we store that information in the brain; and finally, we retrieve that information from the brain. From each of these steps, we can learn something interesting about memory in the modern world.

With regard to memory encoding, more than a century ago psychologist Hermann Ebbinghaus demonstrated that the manner in which we expose ourselves to information has a big impact on how memories are formed. More specifically, Ebbinghaus recognized that when we endeavor to ingest massive amounts of information in a single sitting, we ultimately remember less than when we expose ourselves to that same information over a series of shorter periods — ideally, interspersed with several bouts of sleep. If you've ever pulled an all-night cram session for an exam only to forget everything you studied a week later, you've experienced this principle in action.

Amidst the current attention economy, many modern technologies have been designed to continuously pump out information so as to keep users engaged for longer periods of time. Netflix urges us to watch one more episode, hyperlinks compel us to open one more tab, intermittent rewards drive us to play one more game.

Unfortunately, when information exposure is constant and ceaseless, our ability to hold onto information naturally diminishes. Human beings have always had a limit to the amount of information they could meaningfully encode in any given day. Modern technologies have not changed this; they simply push us beyond this limit more frequently than media of the past.

Here's the problem: in order to meaningfully interact with offloaded information, we must remember where that information is located — which keystrokes are required to access it, how to sift through it, etc. These processes are all internally stored memories. Accordingly, rather than killing our ability to create memories, technology is simply changing what information we choose to remember.

The secret to forming deep, lasting memories resides in the final retrieval phase. Put simply, memory is constructive: the more you retrieve a memory, dredging it up from the depths using your own cognitive faculties, the easier it becomes to recall in the future. This is likely why we remember so many TV jingles — we retrieve these songs each time we sing them — and why we don't remember so many ubiquitous logos — very few of us have ever retrieved these images.

Unfortunately, outside of usernames and passwords, technology is very bad at forcing us to retrieve information. This is the key reason why it may seem technology is killing our memories: when we need never recall information, relevant memories become weak and fleeting. Rest assured, there is no reason to assume human beings are losing the capacity to form deep memories. We are simply using this faculty to access and create deep memories for things such as usernames, passwords, and URLs.

Although technology may be changing what information we encode, store, and retrieve, it does not appear to be altering our memory machinery. The fact that you can remember the name of the folder that holds a specific document, even if you don't remember the contents of that document, shows memory is still chugging along. We are merely employing it differently than previous generations. This leads to the truly important questions: Do we like how we are currently using our memory? Do we like how this may be altering our learning, our discourse, our evolution?

If the answer is "no," then we need to re-evaluate how we are employing modern technologies. That our tools may not be killing memory does not mean they are innocuous.

Adapted from the article written by Jared Cooney Horvath on the-scientist.com

Word Bank

encode	v. convert (information or an instruction) into a particular form 编码
retrieve	v. get or bring (something) back from somewhere 寻回，找回
alter	v. change in character or composition, typically in a comparatively small but significant way 改变
rattle	v. make or cause to make a rapid succession of short, sharp knocking sounds 喋喋不休
digit	n. any of the numerals from 0 to 9, especially when forming part of a number 数字
fade	v. gradually grow faint and disappear 逐渐消失
capability	n. the power or ability to do something 能力
acquainted	adj. having fair knowledge of 熟悉
psychologist	n. an expert or specialist in psychology 心理学家
endeavor	v. try hard to do or achieve something 尽力，竭力
ingest	v. absorb (information) 获取（某事物）
ultimately	adv. finally; in the end 最后；最终
intersperse	v. scatter among or between other things; place here and there 散布，散置
bout	n. a short period of intense activity of a specified kind 一阵
cram	v. study intensively over a short period of time just before an examination 死记硬背功课；临时准备应考
intermittent	adj. occurring at irregular intervals; not continuous or steady 间歇的
ceaseless	adj. constant and unending 不停的
keystroke	n. a single depression of a key on a keyboard, especially as a measure of work 按键
sift	v. examine (something) thoroughly so as to isolate that which is most important 筛选；过滤
reside	v. be situated 在于
constructive	adj. having or intended to have a useful or beneficial purpose 建设性的
dredge	v. bring something unwelcome and forgotten or obscure to people's attention cognitive faculty 重提；翻出；回忆
fleeting	adj. lasting for a very short time 转瞬间的

新理念雅思口语教程
A Transformative Course Book: IELTS Speaking

chugging	*n.* make a series of muffled explosive sounds 发出（持续而单调的）短声
discourse	*n.* written or spoken communication or debate 演说
evolution	*n.* the gradual development of something 演变；进化；发展
innocuous	*adj.* not harmful or offensive 无害的

Task 1 *Read the article and tick the best choice.*

1. What are the three steps in the process of memory?

   A) Encoding, storing, retrieving.

   B) Receiving, encoding, storing.

   C) Encoding, retrieving, outputting.

   D) Encoding, storing, outputting.

2. Which statement is TRUE about people's ability to hold onto information?

   A) The ability decreases as people grow older.

   B) Women tend to encode more information than men at a time.

   C) People can only encode a limited amount of information.

   D) Technology enhances people's ability to encode information.

3. Why can't people remember logos well?

   A) Because they have problem encoding such information.

   B) Because they seldom retrieve such information from brain.

   C) Because they are naturally good at remembering sounds.

   D) Because the logos are too difficult to remember.

4. Which statement is NOT TRUE about technology?

   A) It doesn't change people's memory machinery.

   B) It alters the way how people use memory.

   C) It is killing our memory gradually.

   D) It constantly challenges people to the amount of information they could encode.

Task 2 *Please share ideas with your partners about the following questions based on what you read.*

1. What can individuals do to prevent the negative impacts of technology to memory?

2. Is it a good idea for workplace and school to restrict the use of social media? Why?

Please retell the following short paragraph by using your own words.

The secret to forming deep, lasting memories resides in the final retrieval phase. Put simply, memory is constructive: the more you retrieve a memory, dredging it up from the depths using your own cognitive faculties, the easier it becomes to recall in the future. This is likely why we remember so many TV jingles—we retrieve these songs each time we sing them—and why we don't remember so many ubiquitous logos—very few of us have ever retrieved these images.

Task 4 *Please make a survey among your peers and report the result of your survey in class. You are recommended to do the survey with your group members. The following questions may be included in your survey.*

1. How much time do they spend on social media every day?
2. Do they hold a positive or negative view towards social media? What are the major reasons?
3. If there is a negative impact, what methods did they use to reduce it?

Part Four   Speaking after Listening

IELTS Speaking Skill — ARS: Criteria for Good Argumentation

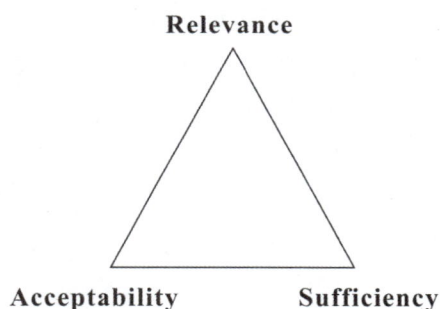

1. Acceptability

Acceptable evidence meet one of the three standards: it is common knowledge; it is supported by a respected publication or an authority, or it is supported by a cogent sub-claim.

e.g. The claim is "AI technology will replace interpretors in the near future." If your evidence is "Anyone who speak two languages can be an interpretor." Then the argument is not valid because the evidence itself is not qualified.

2. Relevance

The standard of relevance is related to the link between evidence and claim. It requires the link successfully connects the evidence to the claim.

e.g. The claim is "AI will make human beings lazy." If your evidence is "Everyone wants to stay in the comfortable zone." Then the argument is not valid because the link is weak between the claim and the evidence.

3. Sufficiency

The standard of sufficiency asks if that link between evidence and claims is good enough to convince the readers.

e.g. The claim is "The prevelance of AI will lead to more diseases among human beings." If your evidence is "AI can help people to do a lot of things." Then the argument is not valid because the evidence given is not enough to support the claim. You should provide more to make the arugment strong.

Task 1 *The following items contain important vocabulary from the lecture "Technology Has Changed How We Communicate". Work with a partner and match vocabulary terms with their definitions. Check your answers in a dictionary if necessary.*

____ 1. Communication tools offer one of the most significant examples of how quickly technology has **evolved**.

____ 2. ... was the best way to communicate **remotely** with someone.

____ 3. ... that affects how people **interact** with each other.

____ 4. Even if you don't use these **platforms**, they're a part of everyday life ...

____ 5. ... whether the **recipient** is right beside you or on the other side of the globe.

____ 6. iMessage has gotten increasingly **sophisticated** over the years.

____ 7. ... technology that captures almost all the **capabilities** of smartphones ...

____ 8. ... allows us to communicate **instantly** with people in our neighborhoods ...

a. (of a machine, system, etc.) clever and complicated in the way that it works or is presented

b. the type of computer system or the software that is used

c. to develop gradually, especially from a simple to a more complicated form

d. immediately

e. from a distance

f. the ability or qualities necessary to do something

g. to communicate with somebody

h. a person who receives something

Task 2 *Listen to a talk about "technology has changed how we communicate", and pick up the best choice.*

1. Which is NOT mentioned as a good way to communicate remotely in the past?

   A) write a letter

   B) sending faxes

   C) use wired telephone

   D) face to face talk

2. What can we infer about social media?

   A) If people do not use them, social media will disappear soon.

   B) Social media take more time if people want to reach someone at distance.

   C) People can send messages in various forms.

   D) Video messages is not popular because the connection can be slow.

3. What is true about messaging apps?

   A) Users can only choose from one or two applications.

   B) Sending videos is not provided by these platforms.

   C) You can use iMessage free of charge.

   D) Messaging apps are not good choices for overseas communication.

4. Which feature down below is exclusive to smartwatches?

   A) Contact friends by sending text messages.

   B) Track personal activities.

   C) Receive notifications from different sources.

   D) Alert emergency assistance when it detects fall.

5. What benefits does NOT technology bring to our life?

   A) It makes our life more colorful.

   B) It allows us to communicate instantly.

   C) It keeps us connected.

   D) It helps us live safer and healthier.

Task 3 *Please paraphrase the following sentence by using your own words.*

Regardless of your location, messages via social media get delivered on these platforms at the same rate and speed whether the recipient is right beside you or on the other side of the globe. You can also send voice messages through these platforms, and it is delivered in nanoseconds.

Task 4 *Please argue the following statements with your partners. Try to use principles of a good argument in the previous part. You can do peer- / or self-assessment by using the criteria below.*

1. Mobile phone has negative effect on people, especially the youngsters.
2. Face-to-face communication is better than communication via internet.
3. A lot of occupations will be replaced by AI in the near future including teacher and interpreter.
4. Technology will change the form of education totally.
5. Government should invest more money to space exploration.
6. Technological innovation is the primary force leading to social development.

Criteria for Peer- / Self-Assessment

NO.	Analytic Items	Proportion	Peer- /Self-Assessment
1	Fluency (less accidental pauses, short pause length, less self-correction)	20%	
2	Fluency (less accidental pauses, short pause length, less self-correction)	20%	
3	Accuracy (accuracy in using words and expressions, accuracy in grammar use)	20%	
4	Complexity(lexical variety, usage of less frequent vocabulary, syntactic complexity)	20%	
5	Pronunciation (no strong accent, correct stress, liaison, plosion in words and sentences, sounds naturally)	20%	
Total Score (use a 10-point scale)			

Technology Innovation — Trends and Opportunities

Technology is moving at an incredible pace. Yet it is not feasible to summarize the trends of technology and opportunities for innovation in a single article. Instead, there are some exciting areas to watch — the most promising developments in the wider information technology spectrum.

1. Artificial Intelligence

Everybody is talking about Artificial Intelligence these days. And yes, in many cases, the topic is covered with exaggerations and hype. Fortunately, the overall A.I. progress and the pace of the underlying technological innovation easily justifies this hype. Consider the progress achieved in fields like Deep Learning and areas such as Computer Vision and Natural Language Processing.

Computer vision is making huge steps, with massive applications in autonomous cars, navigation, robotics, pattern recognition, medical diagnosis, and more. Language Understanding has made tremendous progress as well — recently reached the levels of human understanding — Microsoft reports a word error rate of 5.9% which is equal to human performance on the same input.

Digital assistants become more and more intelligent, contextual, and proactive. At some point in the near future, your digital assistant will be able not only to handle your tasks and information requests but also to do respond with humor — and this will be a major milestone for A.I.

Your digital assistant will know (and keep learning) the style of your humor and how it depends on the time of day, the day of the week, the social arrangement, the agenda of the day, and your implicitly quantified mood. Your digital assistant will be able to make decisions such as when to respond with humor when to proactively say something funny or trigger a humorous dialogue — while always capturing its success via your responses (or lack of). It's coming and it will be fun.

2. Virtual reality

The virtual reality (VR) technology is exploding. So are the opportunities for innovative experiences, use-cases, and products. Content creation for VR is a great opportunity with significant startup activity worldwide. VR startups are working across multiple domains and business scenarios, including E-commerce, gaming, social applications, learning and education, healthcare, online VR environments, and more. The next few years will bring impressive progress on all VR hardware, applications, and VR content.

3. Augmented reality

Augmented reality is what we get when physical and digital worlds blend into a single experience. Typical examples are Microsoft HoloLens and Google Glass. Again, this is an area that will grow rapidly as the opportunity for innovation is unlimited: content experiences, content discovery, data exploration and visualizations, intelligent and contextual object annotation, dynamic physical world mapping and discovery, industrial applications for field workers — are just some examples of the applications which will empower the ways we understand our world.

4. Analytics and visualization

Data availability has exploded — modern corporations have access to vast amounts of complex data, both internal and from the public domain. The breadth and depth of data available require new ways to summarize, visualize, and present data. Novel ways to experience data and insights could involve intelligent interactive synopsis and "data navigation" systems, VR and AR experiences, voice-driven insights discovery, and "personalized data exploration" scenarios. I do believe that there are great new ways to visually browse and understand data, discover and explore hidden structures, trends, and patterns.

5. Robotics

Robots are already here, in one form or another. Regardless of the particular class — humanoids, nano-robots, military, industrial, and so on — the progress is impressive. On one hand, it is the advances in terms of hardware, sensors, and operating software; on the other hand, it is the progress of Artificial Intelligence which makes it possible to integrate cognitive services and dramatically increase Robot's capabilities for real-time decision making.

In the near future, we will start to meet Robots with proactive behaviors, advanced context understanding, able to adapt to human sentiment, enforce 'personalities' and communication styles.

Technology innovation can take many forms — for instance, novel software implementing new algorithms and data processing models; or new hardware components (sensors, processors, components); or improved user interfaces offering seamless experiences; it can also happen at a higher level, in the form of new processes, business models, monetization engines, and so on.

Adapted from the article by George Krasadakis published on medium.com

Task 1　*Read the article and introduce one of the areas in information technology to your partners by using your own words. You can refer to the information in the article, and jot down the key points in the following box.*

| |
| |

Task 2　*Illustrate the main characteristics about each promising area of information technology. Give details for each main point and fill the form below.*

1	Artificial Intelligence	
2	Virtual Reality	
3	Augmented Reality	
4	Analytics and Visualization	
5	Robotics	

Task 3   *Tell your partner which of the above-mentioned information technology you think is the most promising one and explain why.*

From my perspective, ... is the most promising field.

This is because ...

Task 4   *Listen to a lecture about "How Technology Changes Our Sense of Right and Wrong" and choose the correct meaning of each word in bold.*

_____ 1. In an era of extreme **polarization**, it's really dangerous to talk about right and wrong.

_____ 2. ... those who think you're wrong may burn you at the **stake** or ...

_____ 3. ... there was a work by extraordinary **abolitionists** who risked their lives ...

_____ 4. A single barrel of oil contains the energy **equivalent** of the work of five to 10 people.

_____ 5. You can quit **oppressing** people and have a doubling in lifespan ...

_____ 6. Technology changes the way we interact with each other in **fundamental** ways.

_____ 7. You tried to leave the **trench** in the other direction.

_____ 8. ... if you even **quibble** with me, then you're wrong ...

_____ 9. ... simply because our **notions**, our understanding of right and wrong change across time.

_____ 10. This is not a time to continue **ripping** nations apart.

a. a conception of or belief about something

b. division into two sharply contrasting groups or sets of opinions or beliefs

c. tear or pull (something) quickly or forcibly away from something or someone

d. a person or thing that is equal to or corresponds with another in value, amount, function, meaning, etc.

e. a wooden post to which a person was tied before being burned alive as a punishment

f. a person who favors the abolition of a practice or institution, especially capital punishment or (formerly) slavery

g. argue or raise objections about a trivial matter

h. keep (someone) in subjection and hardship, especially by the unjust exercise of authority

i. a long, narrow ditch dug by troops to provide a place of shelter from enemy fire

j. forming a necessary base or core; of central importance

Task 5 *Listen to a lecture again and fill the following sentences according to what you hear.*

1. And that means that those who think you're wrong may _____ or those who are on your side that think you're not _____ may try and cancel you.

2. One of the greatest wrongs, _____, indentured servitude, which was something that was practiced for millennia.

3. You can _____ people and have a doubling in lifespan after _____ for millennia.

4. And there's almost no _____ to meet each other, to try and find some sort of a _____ between right and wrong.

5. In these polarized times, I'd like to revive two words you rarely hear today: _____ and _____.

Task 6 *Choose one of the areas from the passage and think about the positive and negative effects of it. Then fill in the form below.*

Area	Positive Effects	Negative Effects

Task 7 *Share your idea with your partners about one of the following statements.*

1. It has become appallingly obvious that our technology has exceeded our humanity.

2. If we continue to develop our technology without wisdom or prudence, our servant may prove to be our executioner.

3. Technology is a powerful force in our society. Data, software, and communication can be used for bad: to entrench unfair power strustures, to undermine human rights, and to

protect vested interests. But they can also be used for good: to make underrepresented people's voice heard, to creat opportunities for everyone, and to avert disasters.

Part Six   Encountering IELTS Speaking

Words and Expressions about Technology and Innovation

electronic devices 电子设备

technology 科技

high tech 高科技

techie 电脑迷 / 科技迷

advances 进步

indispensable 必不可少的

social media 社交媒体

technophobe 害怕 / 讨厌科技的人

device 设备

online 在线的，线上的

software 软件

upgraded 升级

modern 现代的

gadgets 小机械；小器具

user-friendly 方便用户的

Internet safety 网络安全

Internet security 网络安全

computers 电脑

websites 网站

browse 浏览

laptops 便携式电脑

wifi hotspots 无线热点

surf the Internet 上网浏览信息

technophile 技术爱好者

tech-savvy 熟悉科技的

progress 进步，发展

innovation 创新

innovative 创新的

revolutionary 革命性的；彻底的

revolutionize 革命；彻底改变

breakthrough 突破

modify 修改；更改

cutting-edge 尖端的

state-of-the-art 艺术级的

outdated 过时的

obsolete 陈腐的；老旧的

impact 影响；冲击

transform 改变

game changer 游戏规则改变者

affect 影响

computer literate 能使用计算机的

computer buff 电脑迷

word processing 文字处理

hardware 硬件

crash（电脑）死机

viral 快速传播的

e-commerce 电子商务

e-book 电子书

privacy 隐私

censorship 审查

hacker 黑客

computer virus 电脑病毒

cyber 网络的

cybercrime 网络犯罪

cyber security 网络安全

labour-saving device 节约人力的设备

microchip 微型集成电路片

the digital age 数字时代

appliance 器具；装置

nanotech 纳米科技

enterprise software 企业级软件

AI (Artificial Intelligence) 人工智慧

AR (Augmented Reality) 增强现实

VR (Virtual Reality) 虚拟现实

IoT (Internet of Things) 物联网

IoE (Internet of Everything) 万物互联

ICT (Information and Communication Technology) 信息通信技术

IM (Instant Message) 即时通信

wearable 可穿戴的

big data 大数据

robot 机器人

science and engineering 科学和工程

rank first in the world 全球第一

hot field 热门领域

artificial organ 人造器官

pioneer 先锋

new breakthrough 新的突破

new particle 新粒子

research institute 研究所

sharing economy 共享经济

shared car 共享汽车

shared bike/ bicycle 共享单车

scan the QR code to unlock a bike 扫码解锁单车

illegal parking 违规停车

parking lot/area 停放点

outbound trips/ oversea travelling 出境游

duty-free shop 免税店

overseas shopping 海外购物

mobile payment 移动支付

best place for science and innovation 科技创新宝地

high-speed train 高铁

income distribution 收入分配

market economy 市场经济

artificial intelligence 人工智能

private cars 私人汽车

the negative influence of mass media 大众传媒负面影响

disposable plastic bags 一次性塑料袋

globalization 全球化

the Belt and Road Initiative 一带一路倡议

fulfill one's potential 发挥潜能

improve the efficiency 提升效率

IELTS Speaking Skill — Types of Evidence

When supporting your claim, you are supposed to adopt sufficient evidence. Various types of evidence can help you to develop a solid argument so that you get better chance to convince others. Evidence for persuasion comes in five forms.

1. Data

Data is the type of evidence used most often in presentations. Data are the statistics and facts that have put so many of us to sleep in the course of someone else's presentation. You need to remember that data is one type of evidence among many, and it's not the most effective type. When you're preparing the presentation, pull all the facts and statistics together, then choose a few of your most powerful to present. Keep the rest for the question-and-answer period.

2. Expertise

This is the opinion of someone your audience will accept as an authority on the subject — an expert, in other words. Expert opinion is valuable if you have it. That's one of the reasons they often bring in expert witnesses during the trial phase of Law & Order.

3. Cases/Examples

This type of evidence is most useful when you have examples that are close to the experience of your audience members or particularly meaningful to them. Cases or examples are particularly apt with business audiences because they show real world applications that are easy to understand. Sometimes they even provide a hint of competitive pressure.

4. Image

This is a way of relating a new thing (your recommendation) to something familiar. Image is an explanatory form of evidence; it doesn't prove anything. To say that your new centralized production plan operates like the solar system, with Department X in the center, is just a way to help the audience visualize it. Analogies work very well when acceptance of the recommendation requires some learning.

5. Story

This is something from your personal experience. It may not readily prove your contentions, but it brings them to life. Handled well — which is to say, with authenticity — it can be the most powerful form of evidence.

Task 1 *Think about the claim that the Chinese unicorn company DJI successfully leads the field because of encouraging technological innovation. Support the claim by using at least 2 types of evidence. You can refer to the following outline. Share ideas with your partners.*

Statistics show that ...

It is said that ...

A good case in point is that ...

Task 2 *Think about the claim that "the drone use in daily life will cause more diseases among the public". Support the claim by using at least 2 types of evidence. You can refer to the following outline. Share ideas with your partners.*

Just imagine in the future, ...

According to a survey, ...

For example, ...

From my own experience, ...

IELTS Speaking Test Items

Part 1

1. Do you think it's important to reply e-mails quickly?
2. How often do you send e-mails?
3. Do you prefer to write by hand or on a computer?
4. Do you think computers might one day replace handwriting?
5. What are the disadvantages of social networking apps?
6. Why do you use social networking apps?
7. How often do you use these apps?
8. Has the Internet made your job/studies easier?
9. Have you ever bought anything online?
10. How much time do you spend using a computer at work or at home?

▶ **Sample Answer**

2. How often do you send e-mails?

I probably write between 5 and 10 work e-mails every day, and I send e-mails to friends or family a few times a week.

3. Do you prefer to write by hand or on a computer?

It depends what I'm doing. I prefer the computer for most things because it's faster and you can save or copy things, but I still like making notes or writing ideas down by hand.

4. Do you think computers might one day replace handwriting?

No, I think we will always write by hand as well. I think it's an important skill, and schools will continue to teach children to write by hand before they learn to type.

Part 2

1. Describe a website you use that helps you a lot in your work or studies.

You should say:

What the website is;

How often you use the website;

What information the website gives you;

And explain how your work or studies would change if this website didn't exist.

2. Talk about some technology that you have started using fairly recently.

You should say:

What it is and what it does;

How it makes life better or easier;

How it is different to other similar technology;

And say whether you think you will still be using it in ten years' time or not, and why.

3. Describe your favorite gadget.

You should say:

What is it;

When did you get it;

How often do you use it;

And say why is it so important to you.

▶ **Sample Answer**

I don't own many gadgets. I have a PC, laptop and a smartphone and I can't imagine my life without either of those. However, my laptop is the most important piece of technology for me. I got it as a birthday present from my parents a few years ago and I use it nearly every day now. Although at first using it was like rocket science for me, after a few weeks I was able to do everything I needed, from browsing websites to reinstalling the operating system. What's more, without my laptop I wouldn't be able to do my homework for the university. Also, I use it for surfing the Internet and finding whatever I want, whether it is a piece of code for my project or a useful tip on how to cook a steak. Generally, my laptop became an essential device for me.

4. Describe a time when you started using a new technological device (e.g. a new computer or phone)

You should say:

What device you started using;

Why you started using this device;

How easy or difficult it was to use;

And explain how helpful this device was to you.

Part 3

1. Do you think men and women view technological devices differently?
2. What technology or equipment is used in most workplaces nowadays?
3. Does technology help workers or make their lives more difficult?
4. What effect does new technology have on employment?
5. How much has technology improved how we communicate with each other?
6. Do you agree that there are still many more major technological innovations to be made?
7. Could you suggest some reasons why some people are deciding to reduce their use of technology?

▶ **Sample Answer**

1. Do you think men and women view technological devices differently?

   Yes, I do. For starters, men are usually more obsessed with gadgets. They are almost like children with the way they want to play with the latest gizmos and learn all their new functions. They are constantly fiddling around with their new toys. I also think that gadgets are a kind of ego for men. I mean they often compare their new toys with each other to see who has the best one. Women, on the other hand, are more down to earth and see devices more rationally as a means to communicate with others or to perform a particular function. Of course, this is pretty stereotyped but it seems to hold true for most men and women I know.

3. Does technology help workers or make their lives more difficult?

   Technology definitely helps workers because it makes many tasks so much easier. For example, e-mail is such a useful tool for communication between employees in different offices, or even in different countries. On the other hand, technology can make life more difficult, especially when it goes wrong. It causes a lot of stress when the Internet is down or a computer crashes.

Checklist for This Chapter

Please check according to the scale from 1 to 5.

(1 — Strongly Disagree; 2 — Disagree; 3 — Undecided; 4 —Agree; 5 — Strongly Agree)

Can-do List	1	2	3	4	5
I can talk about topics about technology.					
I am familiar with question types in Speaking.					
I can use ARS strategy in argumentation.					
I can use different evidence to support my opinion.					
I can develop critical thinking on the development of technology.					

Self-reflection

1. In which part have I done very well?

2. In which part should I make improvement?

3. What should I do to bridge the current gap?

4. What suggestions do I have for my teacher or the class arrangement?

5. Anything I would like to say.

(Your reflection could be written in Chinese)